LAND USES
In American Cities

by

Harold M. Mayer
The University of Wisconsin-Milwaukee

and

Charles R. Hayes
The University of North Carolina
at
Greensboro

Park Press
2612 N. Mattis Ave.
Champaign, Illinois
61820

Delray Beach   Greensboro   Champaign

Geography Editor: D. Gordon Bennett
Graphics: Maggie L. Hayes
Cover: Roberta S. Hayes
Media Consultant: Charles L. Hodgin
Production: Homeaco Design of Greensboro

Library of Congress Catalog Number 82-81036 ISBN   0-941226-02-6

Preface

The authors acknowledge the volume and complexity of the material available on urbanism and realize the futility of attempting to teach "Urban Geography" in a one semester undergraduate course. We believe that an introduction to urban land use (the internal structure of cities) is quite enough for one course. We have, accordingly, kept this book short, simple, and to the point. This book is suggested for a one semester or single quarter beginning course in **Urban Land Use** or, it can be used in conjunction with other texts. Thus, many topics have been omitted and none pursued in depth.

Many terms referring to cities are ambiguous, especially given the realities of recent migration patterns. The terms city, urban, etc. are used to encompass the entire urbanized area. The term central city means administrative city to us and suburbs are satellite population clusters within metropolitan boundaries. We refer to population clusters outside metropolitan boundaries as exurbs, satellites, or counter-urbanized areas. With the spread of population from cities, the dichotomy of "urban" and "rural" is less meaningful now than in the past.

Contents

Graphics

Tables

CHAPTER ONE

Introduction:
The Nature of Urban Geography

With the rapidly increasing proportion of the population of the world, both in the developed countries and in the "emerging" or lesser developed nations living and working in cities, towns and villages, as contrasted to the rural or non-urban population, geographers have, for several decades, increasingly focused their attention upon the geography of urban areas. During the two centuries since the United States was established as a nation, the proportion of the American people living in "urban places" — identified by the Census as places with a population of at least 2,500 — has increased from slightly over five percent at the time of the first census in 1790 to almost eighty percent in 1980.

What is meant by the term "urban"? Unfortunately, the perception of "urban" differs from person to person. To some, it refers to cities, and especially large cities; to others it implies the existence and concentration of many problems which are associated with those areas having high population density, and, commonly, to areas of tension, including racial tension. We must be very careful to distinguish, since most Americans live in urban areas, those problems which are problems of the total society from those which are related specifically to urban places as specific forms of man's occupance of the land. Wherever large numbers of people are located, one can expect a concentration of problems, but urban areas, in themselves, do not cause or exacerbate all of the problems of a society.

"Urban", as we consider the term in this book, refers specifically to cities, and by extension to smaller urban places, characterized by a relatively high concentration of people and physical facilities, such as manufacturing, wholesale and retail trade, communication and transportation, government, education, and certain types of recreation and entertainment which can most effectively be carried out when people and facilities are in mutual proximity.

Regardless of the function, it must take place somewhere: it occupies land. Each function takes place in one or more *establishments,* each establishment having a specific location and occupying a specific *site.* Each site-function is connected, by systems of transportation and communication, with the other sites, and the *pattern* of location of functions and of the people and facilities for carrying on the functions, including residence, is the spatial organization of land uses, the topic which this book concerns itself.

Geography is both an academic and an applied field which, more than any other discipline, is primarily, almost uniquely, concerned with the spatial patterns of activities and land uses. Like its counterpart, history, it has no special subject matter. Any phenomena, both tangible such as buildings, roads, and, of course people, and intangible such as cultural traits, languages, religions, and perceptions, which are non-ubiquitous — that is, unevenly distributed spatially — are amenable to historical and geographical investigation. History is primarily concerned with changes — temporal non-ubiquities — through time; geography is primarily concerned with spatial non-ubiquities. But geography also has a time dimension. If we are to understand contemporary spatial patterns, as, for example, the locations and inter-relations among the land uses in a city, we must have some knowledge of how they originated, how they changed through time, and how they may further change in the future. Thus, some geographers are primarily historical geographers, and the sub-discipline of historical urban geography attracts an increasing number of practitioners and students of geography and allied fields; historical preservation and reconstruction of buildings, and here and there entire city neighborhoods, is an important application of the field. On the other hand, the changes in cities in the past may be valuable indicators of what may happen in the future, and could furnish some guidance in the formulation and effectuation of policies for the future development of cities.

Unlike some of their predecessors of generations past, modern geographers, for the most part, have repudiated the idea of environmental determinism, that is, the concept that man can do little if anything to affect the influence of his natural environment upon his future. For a while the pendulum swung in the opposite direction: toward cultural determinism, to the extent that man can completely control his own destiny. Now, the prevalent attitude is that, up to a point, societies can control their futures, within the constraints of certain environmental conditions. The "principle of least effort" implies that it is easier to utilize among alternative paths to human goals the alternative among a set of alternatives which involves the least expenditure of time, money and energy: "design with nature" rather than trying completely to overcome it. Increasingly, environmental considerations must be involved in the processes of planning for the future. Since passage of the national Environmental Protection Act in 1969, detailed environmental impact statements are required for official approval of numerous kinds of projects and programs, both in the public sector and in the private sector. Urban land uses impact upon one another; this principle was recognized in comprehensive zoning, following the first city to adopt it — New York in 1916 — and the declaration of its constitutionality by the Supreme Court of the United States in 1926. Consideration of urban land uses and their mutual interactions must, therefore, involve considerations of the complexities of the total urban environment, both physical and social. The geographers of the recent past, some of whom developed elaborate mathematical models of hypothetical sets of conditions have, themselves, come to the realization that the variables affecting man and his environment are extremely complex, and that the anomolies — the observations which do not conform to the models — are as significant as the models themselves. The models tend to be stochastic ones — that is, they describe probabilities, rather than definite, predetermined and invariable conditions.

Thus, nature does not determine the characteristics, including the spatial patterns and internal land use structures, of cities; they are the result of decisions made in the past by individuals, groups, and governmental policies and actions. It follows, then, that if one selects among the available alternatives toward a goal those policies and actions which "design with nature" or follow the most efficient path, the chances of success are maximized.

This process of selection from alternative paths toward goals, and the implementation of actions along such paths, is the essence of planning. Planning — of neighborhoods, cities, counties, regions, and the nation — is engaged in by many people, but it has become a distinct, organized, academic and applied discipline in its own right. Many geographers find satisfying and constructive — and sometimes lucrative — careers in planning. Urban planning constitutes a major applied field in which the concepts of geography are utilized.

One statement about the realm of planning, including urban planning, is that it concerns itself with the continuum between the inevitable and the impossible. If the future is inevitable, planning would be futile; on the other hand if achieving the goals is impossible there is also no use for planning.

Most geographers implicitly make the assumption that almost anything is possible. It is much easier to achieve if the laws and conditions of nature are utilized, but the limits to human achievement — given sufficient incentive — which may be economic, political, humanitarian, military — almost any goal could be reached if sufficient resources, including human effort, are brought to bear. There is, in most instances, almost an infinity of options available, some of which are more practicable than others. The planner, in making his recommendations, must indicate the principal options, and the advantages and disadvantages of adopting each of them. In this process, the geographer may play a vital role, by contributing his understanding and insight relative to the variables pertinent to the problems. In urban planning, the knowledge of the spatial aspects of urban land uses, including their mutual interrelationships, is a major component of the sub-discipline of urban geography, which, in turn is — or could be — a significant contributor to the process of urban and regional planning.

CHAPTER TWO

Urban Space Consumption

Urban Development

Fixed settlements have existed in the world for some 10,000 years. Social scientists differ concerning the reasons for city formation, but several possible reasons can be generalized.

One historic reason for city formation is defense. It was easier for clusters of people to defend themselves against outside enemies than for individuals to attempt the same thing. Therefore, in many instances city formation may have been for reasons of physical defense. In the nuclear era, dispersion rather than concentration may constitute more effective defense, but many defense activities still require concentrations of people and facilities. With dispersion, lines of communication and transportation are vulnerable to attack and sabotage.

A second reason for city formation is the need to create a process center for raw materials originating in the surrounding area. A group of people can divide jobs both by process and product and produce an item at less cost than can one person attempting to produce the entire product. This division of labor leads to an heterogeneity of skills and ultimately to scale economies.

A third reason for city formation is the need for central places to act as markets for collection of goods and the wholesale and retail distribution of goods and services.

Another reason for city formation is for control and administration of the surrounding area. Taxes can be collected and laws enforced more easily from a central point.

Finally, cities may develop for cultural reasons. People simply like to live in or near cities and have, apparently, for some 10,000 years.

There are several reasons, then, for city formation, but why the rush to the city? One important reason for urban explosion, or perhaps it should be termed urban implosion, is economic. Wages and salaries were higher in cities than in rural areas or small towns. It is true that the cost of living was also higher in cities, but it has been pointed out many times that the result was a higher standard of living within, as opposed to outside, metropolitan boundaries.

A second reason for the rapid rate of urbanization from 1850 to 1970 was social. There were more things to see and do in the city. Restaurants, theaters, night clubs, museums, art galleries, professional sports, and so on, were available in the city and limited or non-existant in the rural areas and small towns of the country. The city offered more amenities. When people lived close together, it was possible to have more social contacts with greater facility.

Social scientists also differ with each other on the steps in urban development. In fact, there are nearly as many theories as there are scholars. Again, however, certain key steps in the development of cities can be generalized.

The first settlements must have been founded as a result of a population explosion some 10,000 years ago. There is not agreement on whether the increased population resulted from the domestication of plants or whether the population explosion required the domestication of plants. Either way, city formation surely depended on the existence of a sedentary population, and a sedentary population generally depends upon agriculture, although there are certain other activities that also support sedentary people.

An early step in the development of an urban unit from a physical agglomeration of people was probably the emergence of full time specialists. With division of labor, cooperation and social interaction become necessary.

Another early step in urban development was probably taxation. Taxes were extracted to support a king or deity, but they concentrated surplus, resulting in capital accumulation sufficient to provide essential services and the physical artifacts typical of cities. Taxation also required record keeping; hence mathematics, written language, and record keeping specialists. Surely a few of these specialists had time to speculate and think, thus stimulating science, technology, and the arts.

Steps one and two would certainly result in the next step: social control. It was necessary, at some point, to have social control so that order could be maintained and so that the urban system would function smoothly. Many social scientists believe that a city should be defined in terms of social control. Others believe that size and density offer better criteria for urban definition.

Human beings have been living in cities for many years. However the industrial revolutions are really responsible for the modern urban explosion especially in North America, Europe and Japan. There have been three industrial revolutions so far. The first two revolutions started in western Europe and spread to the United States. The third industrial revolution, still under way, started in America and is spreading to Europe.

The steam and iron revolution began in Western Europe in the late 18th century and spread quickly to the United States. Prior to that time manual power, water power and animal power made it more efficient to produce manufactured goods in small, widely dispersed units; the cottage industry. Each stream or person could be exploited for small amounts of power so industry located where people were and people located at the source of food or raw materials.

It should be pointed out that there have been real advantages to agglomeration; to city growth. It has been pointed out that specialization and division of labor leads to scale economies. There are, however, other scale economies of agglomeration. For example, the possibility of maintaining common inventories, and sub-contracting certain manufacturing processes both lead to economy of scale. Perhaps the most important scale economy resulting from agglomeration is the potential for generation and transmission of ideas and innovation, which is facilitated by face to face contact. High densities are necessary for efficient transportation and communication, which in turn is essential for distribution of goods and services. Transport cost is a fundamental element of location. The steam and iron revolution accentuated these agglomerative forces, thus accelerating city growth.

The second industrial revolution might be called the mechanical revolution. The mechanical revolution developed in Western Europe in the mid-nineteenth century and soon spread to the United States. This revolution depended on the conveyor belt assembly line, direct transmission of mechanical power, and interchangeable parts. Although these developments were first combined in western Europe, it was an American, Henry Ford, who first applied them to large-scale manufacturing in the United States early in the twentieth century.

The mechanical revolution created mass production. Mass production offered goods to the consumer at reduced prices and created more consumers, which in turn created more jobs, which further reduced prices and so in a circular and cumulative fashion. The factories attracted people to the city. They required services, giving rise to a wide variety of commercial and public services and institutions.

The third industrial revolution can be variously termed "the electronic revolution", the "computer revolution" or "automation." Whatever it is called, it started in the United States after World War II, spread to western Europe and around the world. Although the full impact of automation is yet to be felt, certain trends are already evident. The electronic revolution has increased the number, variety and level of skills necessary for success in individual and organization competition. Some people do not have or are not motivated to acquire these higher skills. There tends to be a discrepancy between available people and available jobs. We recognize this and call it technological unemployment. The electronic revolution has produced machines that supplant workers in certain one-industry cities and regions. This constitutes geographic unemployment. If these trends continue, there will surely be talented, well educated or well trained people who cannot find jobs. A two-fold problem results from this: (1), how do we transfer the title to consumption (i.e. money) to these people, and who bears the burden; and (2), how will it be possible for these people to feel like useful contributing members of society?

The electronic revolution has been a force for both urban agglomeration and dispersion. The computer is freeing society from conventional files, but not from communication. Since machines work and people think in a computerized society, we are moving from a supervisional to a transactional society. Idea generation and idea and information exchange are becoming more important functions in modern society. Face-to-face contact can enhance these functions and face-to-face contact is facilitated by concentrations of people in cities. Nevertheless, our definition of "city" is changing as people move outward to and beyond the periphery in unprecedented numbers. Nevertheless, a high proportion of Americans is destined to live in and near cities. The problem is how to live happily. Perhaps the outward movement discussed in the next section is an attempt to learn to live happily in the urban environment.

The industrial revolutions have resulted in significant changes in city structure and have modified intra-city growth. Pre-industrial cities were primarily government, defense, religious and educational centers. Only secondarily were they commercial and processing centers. Pre-Industrial cities exhibited little specialization of land use; a single site commonly served several functions. Industrial cities on the other hand are characterized by a high degree of land use specialization.

The morphology (spatial form) of the pre-industrial city centered the religious, administrative, and commercial nodes. These were surrounded by the homes of the wealthy and powerful. Beyond this were the homes and work-shops of the craftsmen, and beyond this lived the poorest of the urban dwellers, sometimes outside the protection of the city wall. The entire arrangement was for protection and was quite static. There was little need for change or growth since cities grew very slowly if at all.

The morphology of the American industrial city is in some ways almost the opposite of the pre-industrial city. The poor tend to live close to the city center, and the more affluent toward and beyond the urban periphery. Although some government, religious, commercial and manufacturing functions are at the city core, many are dispersed throughout the city and beyond. This pattern came about because factories out-bid people for close-in sites, and rich people out-bid poor people for residential sites at a distance from the noxious influence of factories. Anyway, poor people in the pre-industrial city had no transport other than feet, so they were forced to live close to work. Other functions agglomerated near work or residence at first, but as the rich and then the middle-income people began to move outward as the city grew, some functions followed the people.

A partial and very generalized urban migration model, then, would show the more affluent citizens fleeing the central city for the periphery and beyond, leaving the inner city to the less affluent. Although overall urban population densities in the United States have been declining for several decades, densities are still higher closer to the city center and they decline outward. The land value or rent curve exhibits the same pattern as the density curve, but the family income curve shows the opposite trend: that is, average family income tends to increase from the city center outward. Why do the poor people generally live on high priced land and the rich people on low priced land? Transport requires capital, and poor people do not have capital. Transport requires expenditure, and poor people do not have the money to spend. Further, land parcel size is larger farther out (i.e. lower density living) so, although unit cost is less, total cost is more. Thus land costs ("site rentals") and transport costs ("transfer costs") can substitute for each other.

In a notable article many years ago, Charles Colby pointed out that the form of cities results in large part from two opposite forces: centripetal (centralizing) and centrifugal (decentralizing). Both in turn, represent a balance between attractive and repulsive forces in central and peripheral locations. Each activity, establishment or land use, regardless of type, is located where it is as the result of a decision, whether explicit or implicit as to the optimal balance for that establishment or function between central and peripheral location. Of course, inertia — represented by unamortized facilities or other constraints — may result in retention of a given land use for a while after its location is no longer optimal. The balance between centripetal and centrifugal forces in urban location is somewhat analogous to placing an artificial satellite into orbit around the earth: the earth's gravity is the centripetal force; the thrust of the launching rockets represents the centrifugal force. The orbit is the distance from the center of the earth when the two are equal.

The model above describes the usual and the average situation. Nevertheless, we can draw a selected traverse from city center outward that shows an increase in land values outward from the city center. It is necessary to add another factor to account for this phenomenon; the amenity factor.

It is difficult to quantity an amenity factor. Nevertheless, it is possible to generalize on some of the reasons for the amenity value of residential land. High ground and the presence of a pleasant view makes residential land more valuable. The absences of, or at least distance from, noxious influences (i.e. factories, railroads, swamps, etc.) constitute a residential amenity. The presence of people with similar socio-economic backgrounds is regarded by many people as a residential amenity factor, although some prefer to live in neighborhoods with heterogeneous rather than homogeneous population.

DISTANCE DECAY
POPULATION DENSITY and/or LAND VALUES

Fig. 1

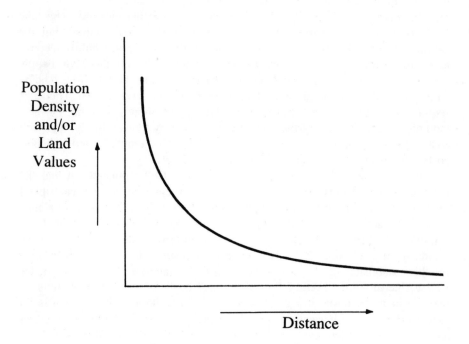

The shape of the curve representing the distance decay of population density and/or land values is termed "negative exponential" or (popularly) "Reverse J." It is evident that population density and land values decrease with distance from the metropolitan center. The shape of the curve representing family income is not yet known. However, so many affluent families have moved outward in the last decade, it is probable that, when data are in and analyzed, the curve will indicate a family income increase with distance from the metropolitan center.

(Homogenity implies not only educational, economic, and social attainment, but skin color and ethnic background.) Access, and the availability of services (i.e. water, sewer, power, garbage collection, shopping centers, good schools, etc.) raises the value of residential land. The presence of highcost housing nearby is a residential amenity factor. In fact, a residence built on a parcel of land can raise or lower the value of that land. Finally, the perceived possibility of re-sale because of the great spatial mobility of the American people constitutes an amenity value for residential land.

The amenity factor is a land value anomoly. A representative land value model would be a profile over the urban areas analogous to the profile of a volcano, with values decreasing outward at a decreasing rate. The amenity factor disturbs this pattern. There are many other land value anomolies, some of which will be considered in further paragraphs.

The industrial revolutions have resulted in rapid urbanization and changes in city form. As urbanization progresses, cities must obviously expand. Many social scientists have attempted to generalize on the growth and expansion of cities. These attempts at generalization are called "urban growth models." We will consider a few of these in the following paragraphs.

Urban Growth

The most famous of the urban growth models is the "concentric zone model" usually credited to Ernest W. Burgess. Although Burgess did not create the model, his writings did publicize it in the United States. The Burgess model states that urban growth is outward from the central business district ("CBD") in concentric rings or zones. Since Burgess associated certain population characteristics or functions with certain zones, the model has been offered as a model of the internal structure of cities. It is not this, it is an empirical urban growth analog with emphasis upon residential areas and inadequate consideration of the locations of industrial and commercial functions.

The Burgess model was modified by Homer Hoyt. The Hoyt "sector model" acknowledges that urban growth may well be outward from the CBD in concentric rings but points out that different parts of each ring may grow at different rates. Thus, growth approximates sectors more than it does rings. The rapidly growing sectors contain high-speed high-capacity radial transport arteries; the slower growing sectors typically do not contain important radial transportation routes. The Hoyt model does not negate the Burgess model. It does modify the Burgess model to the extent that the Hoyt formulation may be considered a separate model.

The Harris and Ullman "multiple nucleii" urban growth model acknowledges both the Burgess and Hoyt models. Harris and Ullman concede that urban growth may be outward in concentric zones or in sectors. However, they

URBAN GROWTH MODELS

Fig. 2

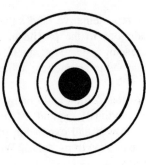

Concentric Zone

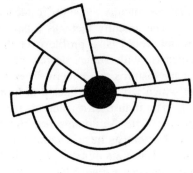

Sector

Multiple Nucleii

Nucleus

The illustration above is a schematic representation of the Burgess, Hoyt, and Harris and Ullman growth models. The models have been deliberately simplified in order to demonstrate the concept. For further information the reader is directed to Harris, Chauncey D. and Ullman, Edward L., "The Nature of Cities", *Annals of the American Academy of Political and Social Science,* Vol. CCXLII (Nov. 1945) pp. 7-17.

point out that growth is not usually from one node, but from many. Growth in concentric zones or sectors would surely occur from the central business district, but it would also occur from other important nodes, such as large shopping centers and manufacturing districts. The multiple nucleii urban growth model is, again, enough of a modification of its predecessors to be considered a separate urban growth model.

These urban growth models have been tested in subsequent research. For example, one investigation found that family size increased outward from the city center in concentric zones while economic status increased outward in sectors. Another found that age of housing and number of occupants per housing unit decreased outward from the city center in concentric zones; housing quality increased outward in concentric zones from multiple nuclei; and the proportion of home owners increased outward from multiple nuclei sectors.

Although the spatial patterns of most American cities represent combinations of the three classical models mentioned previously, the peripheral movement of population and of much business activity from central areas to peripheral areas of cities and beyond has left behind an area of lower density than was formerly present in such areas. This does not necessarily invalidate the three models, but gives rise to a possible additional model, which may perhaps be called the "doughnut" model, with a more-or-less hollow center. In some cities, the hollow was partially filled in by various public urban redevelopment and renewal programs, with varying degrees of success or lack of it. In many cities such programs aborted before completion, thus resulting in extensive areas of inner-city land which are vacant or only partially developed.

Many researchers believe that residential location is a matter of choice and thus urban growth is non-predictable. They acknowledge that the wealthy have more residential choices at their command than do the poor, but, they say, even the poor can choose one slum or another or a rural over an urban slum. It is doubtful, however, that urban growth is completely random and, thus completely non-predictable. Several modern growth prediction methods fit the real world fairly well and thus predict growth to a fair degree of accuracy.

There are many stochastic (probabilistic) models for the predication of urban space consumption and thus urban growth. Many of these models have never been tested because data are unavailable. Others have been tested but because of unreliable data the tests are inconclusive.

Computer simulation models have also been constructed and run in order to predict residential space consumption and thus urban growth. These models also suffer from the non-availability of important input data and they share a problem with the stochastic models in that private and political decisions are commonly excluded because of unpredictability.

Urban Migration

Migration to, from, between, and within cities is quite prevalent in the world. In fact, almost half the people in the United States will have moved within a five year period, most of them in or around a city. Not all countries of the world exhibit such movement, but all exhibit it to an extent. Over half the urban dwellers of the world are "in-migrants" (i.e. moved to the city after age 16) and in some cases the ratio exceeds seventy-five per cent.

The period from 1850 to 1970 exhibited such a strong movement to cities that it has been called the age of "galloping urbanization". During this period, the more technologically advanced the country the more it urbanized, because the rush to the city was primarily the result of the industrial revolution. The census of 1920 first showed that the urban population — in cities, towns, and villages of 2,500 or more — constituted more than half of the population of the United States. The primary reason for the rush to the city was the greater availability of jobs and higher incomes in the city relative to rural areas. This was usually a net gain for the migrant in spite of the higher cost of living in a city; urban disposable incomes were higher.

Throughout this period suburbanization also took place. Suburbanization is as old as urbanization. The reason most often given for the move from the city outward to the suburbs was to "upgrade housing." This might mean a bigger or better house, but it might mean other things as well. It could mean a "better" neighborhood, "better" schools, or "better" playmates for the children. It could mean a neighborhood with residents of like skin color, or it could mean a neighborhood with residents of like socio-economic status. Throughout the period migration to the suburbs was mostly by people of upper-middle and upper income status.

Inter-urban migration was also prevalant during the period 1850-1970. Migration from one city to another tended to be toward the larger cities, and to regional capitals (the largest and most important city within a region). The most accepted reason for inter-urban migration has been "employment opportunity." This might mean simply higher wages and salaries, but it might mean the perception of future opportunity. It might mean more status, or it might mean the opportunity to do a different kind of work.

By 1970 the outward movement became so dramatic that it was given a new name: "counter urbanization." It would seem that the three things we thought we could count on, "death, taxes, and galloping urbanization" have been reduced to two. Rapid urbanization is no longer a fact in the United States nor in most other industrial nations of the developed world. Rapid urbanization is still the way of life in lesser-developed nations, but in the more advanced nations it has been replaced by counter urbanization.

Counter urbanization is defined as the movement from within to without metropolitan boundaries. The difference, though, between suburbanization and counterurbanization is the number of people moving and the distance of the moves. So many people in the United States are moving that the larger cities exhibit a net decline in population from one census to the next. Two thirds of the out-migrants are moving beyond metropolitan boundaries. This trend is true to a lesser extent in all the developed nations of the world, but it is generally not so in the underdeveloped world. The outmigrants are mostly white middle and upper income people so the trend has also been termed "white flight." The filling-in of the cities behind the out-migrants has been mostly the "minorities"; typically Black lower income people, and in some cities by recent migrants from Asian nations and by Hispanic-Americans.

The desire to move outward has probably always been present but could not be completely fulfilled until recently. The outward movement desires of Americans and the people of other developed nations are suggested to be as follows:

1. Love of mobility. (Previously suggested)
2. Love of newness. (new houses in new neighborhoods seem more desirable)
3. Love of nature. (since 1850 people have attempted to bring the country to the city in the form of vegetation, etc.)
4. The "birds-of-a-feather" syndrome. (there seems to be a great desire to live among people one perceives to be one's "own kind")

Of the four desires mentioned in the prior paragraph, the chances are the "birds-of-a-feather" desire is the strongest. But what does this mean to most people? Some will define their own kind as "human being" without regard to race, color or creed. People who accept this definition will likely live in a university or cosmopolitan neighborhood. (This concept will be developed in more detail in Chapter Five). Many will define their own kind in ethnic terms. There are still Jewish, Polish, and German, (et. al.) neighborhoods. Most, however, will define their own kind in income and education (socio-economic) terms. In fact, one of the most dramatic effects of counterurbanization has been the "homogenization" of neighborhoods, suburbs, and exburbs. Socio-economically, birds of a feather are indeed flocking together. Another interesting effect of counter-urbanization is the non-city cities the out-migrants are building. The new counter urbanized residential districts look remarkably like urban sub-divisions but are often miles from a central city.

The desires for outward movement have probably always been present, but what has permitted this counter urbanization? The answer is mainly the lower cost and ubiquitous availability of the automobile, with its enormously resulting flexibility in locational choice, and the increasing use of the truck for the transfer of goods. Recent studies indicate that the increased cost of motor fuel will have only minor if any effect upon people's choice of residential location. New technology of electronic communication and entertainment may, in fact, more than compensate for escalation of intra-metropolitan transportation costs. Factories (jobs) moved outward in search of cheaper land, larger parcels of land, lower taxes, less friction, and perhaps a "pastoral scene". The truck permitted this outward move because it has permitted door-to-door direct delivery everywhere. The people followed the jobs and the shopping centers followed the people. In some instances shopping centers anticipated population movement and served as nucleii for residential development. This concept will be developed in more detail in Chapter Seven.

The era of the 1970's, has seen steady decentralization of all but the lowest incomes and the concentration of most new housing, most industry, and much of the commerce in and beyond the urban periphery. It has seen the increasing segregation of socio-economic groups in the outlying areas and the central city inmigration of the poor, mostly Blacks and other minorities. Upper income people have sought areas of choicest environmental amenities plus physical isolation. Middle income people have moved as close as possible to the upper income people. Moderate income people have sought the older suburbs and the lower income people have moved into the inner city. The exceptions to this are the university and cosmopolitan neighborhoods where similarities are intellectual or artistic rather than economic, racial or ethnic, although the latter factors may be present.

Except for a few scattered places amid predominant white populations, and in spite of "open housing" laws, Blacks are generally denied access to upper-middle and upper cost suburbs and exurbs. Real estate salesmen do not show them properties in such areas; and financial institutions tend to be reluctant to loan money to Blacks for home purchase in certain neighborhoods. But, if all else fails, it is possible to simply overprice a house, refuse a lower offer from a Black person but to accept a lower offer from a white person. It must be said, however, albeit cautiously, that there are indications, very recently, that this coalition between home owners, lending institutions, and real estate agencies is beginning to dissolve, and that a few more upper-middle and upper income Black people are being permitted to buy in some of the afore-mentioned places.

Counter urbanization is having, and has already had, a profound effect on the structure of cities and the rural-urban fringe. There are still many unanswered questions. Let us look at some of the questions raised by this dramatic outward movement and make a few guesses.

1. Where will we work? It was pointed out in the mid-forties that there was a high correlation between place of residence and place of work; that is, people lived close to work. Most studies since then noted an increase in the distance of the journey to work. Innovations in transport technology shortened the time involved in the journey to work, although distance has increased. As personal affluence has increased, increases in disposable income were accompanied by decreases in the ratio of transportation expenditure to total expenditure. Is it possible that people will again live closer to work in the

non-city cities that are being built in the rural-urban fringe? As people have followed the jobs are they again moving closer to work? Will development of outlying employment clusters, already well under way, result in multi-nucleated dispersed cities as the predominant pattern?

Recent research suggests that although the journey to work in outlying areas is almost entirely by private auto, it nevertheless, is usually shorter and less time-consuming than the old "commute." Since most counter-urbanized people also work in the outlying area perhaps time will see them again close enough to the workplace so a brisk walk or bracing bicycle ride will get them to the job.

2. Where will we play? As people spread out over the rural-urban fringe will private recreation prevail? The technology is available. Home video entertainment centers, inexpensive vinyl lined swimming pools, premix concrete for backyard courts, and a plethora of competitively priced sports equipment are all within the financial reach of those counter-urbanized people. Trips for recreation will likely to be places of high amenity (mountain, beach et. al.) and to the cores of the large cities.

3. How about energy and pollution? Even though New York City uses half as much energy per capita as the United States as a whole (because of common walls, public transport, et. al.) it is probable that trips to work, to shop, and for recreation will be shorter. What will be the future role of public mass transportation? Will the bicycle become a viable transport medium? Will solar-assisted heating be more feasible where dwellings are spread out? Pollution is largely a matter of agglomeration and concentration. If people and dwellings are spread out enough won't nature help?

4. What will happen to centrally-located housing? To what extent will renewal take place, and how will it affect housing costs? If old neighborhoods are rebuilt through a process called "gentrification", will centrally-located housing be within economic reach of middle-income people and families; how and where will lower-income people find satisfactory living quarters?

5. What will happen to close to the central city core commercial establishments? Will they go out of business, as they always have when a neighborhood exhibits a decline in purchasing power or will revitalization take place in time to help them?

6. How about life-cycle moves? People tend to move outward as they marry and have children in an effort to upgrade housing at those stages in the life cycle. Some of those people move back into the city after children are reared or upon retirement. Statistically, this movement back is a trickle and will remain so if counter-urbanization is a permanent trend. On the other hand, can inner-city schools be improved to induce a stronger centripetal movement?

7. What is the impact of counter-urbanization on small satellite cities and towns? Capital improvements for water, sewer, public health, etc. constitute financial drains on small communities. After amortization, though, these improvements should be economically self-sustaining. To what extent can

economies of scale be effected by inter-governmental cooperation, or, perhaps by creation of metropolitan governments? What will be the future roles of federal and state governments in influencing the administrative, financial, social and physical conditions of urban areas?

8. Will cities again implode in the face of rising fuel cost and potential fuel shortages? This is not likely, except to a very limited degree. The investment in outlying functions and in housing is too great to anticipate a major reversal of the outward movement. People will work, shop, and play close to home (and functions may fill-in even closer to home), and the private auto (albeit smaller, more fuel efficient, and perhaps even alternatively fueled) will remain the primate people mover.

SELECTED READINGS

Bennett, D. Gordon and Hayes, Charles R., "The Social Impact of Movement into the Rural-Urban Fringe," *Geographical Survey,* Vol. 9, No. 4 (Oct. 1980) pp. 8-9.

Berry, Brian J.L., ed. *Urbanization and Counter Urbanization,* London, Urban Affairs Annual Reviews, Sage Publications (1976).

Bourne, Larry S., "Alternative Perspectives on Urban Decline and Population Deconcentration," *Urban Geography,* Vol. 1, No. 1 (Jan-March 1980).

Bourne, Larry S., *Internal Structure of the City: Readings on Space and Environment,* (New York: Oxford University Press, 1971).

Burgess, Ernest W., "The Growth of the City: An Introduction to a Research Project" *Publications of the American Sociological Society,* Vol. 18 1924) pp. 85-97.

Colby, Charles C., "Centrifugal and Centripetal Forces in Urban Geography," *Annals of the Association of American Geographers,* Vol. 23, No. 1 (March, 1933), pp. 1-20.

Goheen, Peter G., *Victorian Toronto,* Chicago, The Unviersity of Chicago, Department of Geography Research Paper No. 127 (1970).

Harris, Chauncy D. and Ullman, Edward L., "The Nature of Cities" *Annals of the American Academy of Political and Social Science,* CCXLII, (Nov. 1945) pp. 7-17.

Harvey, David, *Society, The City and the Space Economy of Urbanism,* Washington, D.C. Association of American Geographers, Resource Paper No. 18 (1972).

Hoyt, Homer, *One Hundred Years of Land Values in Chicago,* Chicago, University of Chicago Press (1933).

Hoyt, Homer, *The Structure and Growth of Residential Neighborhoods in American Cities,* Washington, D.C., Federal Housing Administration (1939).

Jud, G. Donald and Loop, Carl A., "Demographic Change in the Piedmont Triad," Greensboro, N.C., *North Carolina Review of Business and Economics,* (April, 1979) pp. 3-11.

Mayer, Harold M., "A Survey of Urban Geography", Chap. 3 of *The Study of Urbanization* edited by Philip M. Hauser and Leo F. Schnore (New York: John Wiley and Sons, Inc., 1965), pp. 81-113.

Mayer, Harold M., *The Spatial Expression of Urban Growth*, Washington, D.C. Association of American Geographers, Resource Paper No. 7 (1969).

Mayer, Harold M., "Urban Geography" in *American Geography: Inventory and Prospect* edited by P.E. James and C.F. Jones (Syracuse University Press, 1954), pp. 142-166.

Moore, Eric G., *Residential Mobility in the City*, Washington, D.C. Association of American Geographers Resource Paper No. 13 (1972).

Muller, Peter O., *The Outer City*, Washington, D.C. Association of American Geographers Resource Paper No. 75-2 (1976).

Muller, Peter O., *Contemporary Suburban America*, Englewood Cliffs, N.J. Prentice-Hall (1981).

Plane, David A., "The Geography of Urban Commuting Fields: Some Empirical Evidence from New England, *"Professional Geographer*, Vol. 33, No. 2 (May 1981) pp. 182-188.

Russwurm, Lorne H. et. al., *Essays on Canadian Urban Process and Form*, Waterloo, Univeristy of Waterloo, Pub. No. 10 (1977).

Taafe, Edward J., Gauthier, Howard L. and Maraffu, Thomas A., "Extended Commuting and the Intermetropolitan Periphery, *"Annals of the Association of American Geographers*, Vol. 70, No. 3, (Sept. 1980) pp. 313-329.

U.S. Bureau of the Census, *Metropolitan Area Definition, et. al.* (Bureau of the Census Working Paper No. 28) Washington, D.C. (1968).

Wilvert, Calvin H., "The Population Boom in Rural America," *Journal of Geography*, Vol, 79, No. 5 (Sept/Oct. 1980) pp. 194-5.

CHAPTER THREE

Land Use and Planning

The Land Use Decision Process

It could be said that a principal reason for government is to act in the public interest in the allocation of scarce resources. Urban land is a scarce resource, and governmental intervention is often necessary in order that it may be used efficiently. The Anglo-American philosophy of a free market mechanism does not always work well in the determination of land uses. Some private decisions may be harmful to others, but, more important, we only have one planet and cannot permit its destruction, now or for future generations. Therefore society has decreed that some public control must exist.

Location is the most important factor in the determination of urban land uses. Urban land can increase one-hundred-fold in value should it be needed for a specialized and sporadic use such as "Disney World" or for a motel or restaurant to serve a "Disney World." On the other hand, urban land can decrease tenfold in value with the announcement of the intention to create a sanitary landfill nearby. Urban land can increase or decrease in value with a zoning change; i.e. permission to use land for a different purpose, or revocation of such permission. An increase in urban land value due to a relative location change is called a "windfall"; a decrease a "wipe-out." Wipeouts and windfalls usually occur because of changing conditions beyond the control of the individual, yet government normally assumes no responsibility for either.

Government also has not yet solved other problems with regard to the efficient use of urban land. Waterproofing, runoff, retention, flooding, silting, landslides, and stream pollution all affect the use and value of urban land, yet government has largely ignored the reciprocal effects of one with the others. Urban spread tends to result in abandonment rather than recycling of land, and it requires the construction of streets, roads, utilities, parks, and public buildings. Government has not solved this problem. Land is often withheld from the market in anticipation of future urban use which may or may not occur. Government has not solved the potentially blighting effect of unused, leap-frogged, land.

Governmental land use control is most noticable at the local level through zoning. In theory zoning makes sense. In practice zoning is often prostituted as a device catering to the power elite or the majority in the view, at least, of many. Neither group necessarily reflects real consideration for public health, safety, or welfare. Zoning is often improperly applied, perhaps blocking desirable changes, perhaps changing land value to the detriment of the city. Zoning lacks a temporal dimension — it can designate but not dictate. Fiscal zoning (minimum lot size or minimum house size) may perpetuate residential racial segregation. Finally, zoning is not always upheld in the courts, and it fails as a means of land use control each time this occurs.

Zoning ordinances represent use of the ''police power'' delegated to local governments by the state. They consist of text and map. The text details the permitted uses of the land for each category and the map locates the categories or districts. The purpose of zoning is to eliminate or, at least, minimize undisciplined and mutually incompatible land uses and, if certain principles are followed, can accomplish this in spite of its other deficiencies.

Principles for zoning are as follows:

1) Functional compatibility. That is, we don't permit a bar to locate next to a church, or heavy industry adjacent to a residential area.

2) Zoning must be reasonable, logical, and legal. That is, it must recognize trends, note what is already there, conform to street patterns, terrain, drainage, rail lines, etc. and does not violate anyone's constitutional rights.

3) It must make boundaries as short as possible. That is, all districts should be as discrete and compact as possible.

4) It must follow a comprehensive plan; it must be general, not specific. That is, districts and changes must conform to the overall plan or changes will certainly be defeated in court. ''Spot zoning'' is discriminatory, and thus illegal. A zoning ordinance must *not* be construed to be a plan: it is among the devices for effectuating a plan.

Zoning is a much more effective tool for urban land use control if the city subdivision ordinance is sound. The subdivision ordinance controls the form, function, and land uses of new subdivisions whether residential, industrial or commercial. If the ordinance conforms to the comprehensive plan there will be less pressure for zoning changes as the city grows and matures.

The thoroughfare plan is also an aid or a deterrent to zoning. The construction of new streets, roads, and thoroughfares can shape and reshape the city physically and functionally. If the thoroughfare plan, as a component of a comprehensive plan, complements the zoning plan, the impact of new thoroughfare construction, as access and barrier, will be less dramatic or, at least, will have been pre-determined.

There are several special types of zoning that have worked very well in certain specific cases. Some of these are: hazard zoning, planned unit development, conditional use, and restrictive covenant.

Hazard zoning involves flood plains, coasts, slide areas, etc. It can be effective but involves only small amounts of urban land. Nevertheless, wider use of hazard zoning could mitigate many of the negative and sometimes catastrophic effects of inappropriate location with respect to natural and man-made hazards, such as location of high-intensity uses of flood plains.

Planned Unit Development - PUD for short - is a bridge between zoning and subdivision control. It involves planned clustering with common open space for new residential, commercial, industrial or multiple-use subdivisions. The municipality gets a planned development and "free" open space, and the developer gets permission for clustered high-density building and thus a saving, at the same time conforming to the general principles of a comprehensive plan. In spite of much early criticism (i.e. articles entitled "Pud is a Dud,") some recent planned unit developments are excellent examples of space utilization while retaining architectural beauty and personal privacy. The effectiveness of PUD depends on the skill of the landscape architect/designer, and the wise application of planning principles by the developer and the appropriate public agencies.

Conditional Use zoning involves a special permit technique. The developer must submit a total site plan with his request for a zoning change, and the final development must conform to the approved plan. Many city planners are enthusiastic over the effectiveness of conditional use zoning. On the other hand, an excessive number of conditional use permits could invalidate a comprehensive plan.

Restrictive covenant or deed restriction involves building or development restrictions accompanying the deed for the land and almost amounts to a private zoning plan. Restrictions may involve anything which is legal. They are usually more restrictive than the municipal zoning ordinance. Restrictive covenants seem to work well in neighborhoods where pride of ownership and tender loving care are evident and less well in lower income or declining neighborhoods. The largest American city which has never had a comprehensive zoning ordinance - Houston, Texas - depends mainly on enforcement of restrictive covenants for control of land uses.

Zoning, whether public or private, general or special, is under constant attack. Many believe that it is possible to develop a parcel of the planet without being told how the land can be used. The courts have, indeed, sometimes upheld this view. Many believe zoning is not effective as a means of land use control, and, indeed, there are many legitimate criticisms of zoning. Some believe that zoning stifles creativity in architecture and building. Indeed, setbacks, side yard restrictions, street standards, and lack of public open space requirements do restrict building style. Others, however, believe zoning, though not perfect, is the best we have and that chaos would result without it.

In spite of public awareness of zoning, it is probable that public acquisition is a more effective control over urban land than is zoning. Not only does the federal government, for example, own about a third of the land in the nation, but it is estimated that local governments own as much as half of the urban land at any given time. This land is used for streets, roads, thoroughfares, parks, public buildings, universities and other institutions, redevelopment projects under way, public housing, plus tax delinquent acquisition, gifts, and land that has been purchased for future sale. Streets and alleys, alone, account for one-quarter to one-third of the land in most American cities. Not only is acquisition a powerful tool for land control in itself, but many public uses have a tremendous impact on the use and value of adjacent or nearby private land.

There are many ways to categorize the use of urban land, but the simplest and most used system divides urban land into four general classes: residential, industrial, commercial, and institutional. However, there is not universal agreement among cities as to which functions are to be contained in each category.

The residential category accounts for about 30 percent of the land in the typical city. However, the category blurs on specifying when a rooming house or a residential hotel becomes a commercial establishment and therefore a commercial use of the land.

The industrial component accounts for about 8 percent of the land in a typical city. It includes manufacturing plants, warehousing and wholesaling establishments. Transportational uses such as rail lines and yards, port terminals, airports, and the like, are sometimes classified as industrial, but commonly constitute a separate class of land use.

The commercial category involves retail establishments that purvey goods and services. It accounts for about 4 percent of the land in a typical city. Some cities consider stores in office buildings as commercial. Most cities consider medical, dental, veterinary, legal, advertising, et. al. services commercial, some consider these institutional. For example, is a job printing establishment a commercial or a manufacturing use? Even though their functions and physical characteristics are similar, offices of business firms are classified as "commercial" while offices of public agencies are most commonly designated as "public and institutional" or simply "institutional."

The institutional component uses a whopping 35 percent of the typical city's land. It includes parks, public buildings, streets, roads and thoroughfares

(25 to 35 percent of the urban land alone is in street, roads, and thoroughfares) and private institutions. Obviously state supported universities and private liberal arts colleges qualify, as does a city hall, but how should a for-profit business or secretarial training school be classified? There is no generally accepted principle.

The municipal boundaries rarely coincide with the edge of the built up area. Most commonly, cities are "underbounded" with the urban area "over-spilling" into adjacent incorporated suburban cities, towns, villages, and boroughs." On the other hand, some cities are "overbounded" and contain extensive non-urban land within their incorporated areas. Many cities are underbounded in some directions from the city center and overbounded in other directions. Thus, the proportion of land within municipalities devoted to type of use is dependent, among other factors, on the locations of the municipal boundary relative to the edge of the built-up urban area.

As a generality however, 75 percent to 80 percent of the land in a city is in use; 20 percent to 25 percent is unused. This unused land may be under water or in swamp and thus unusable, or it may involve steep slopes, unsuitable or difficult foundation conditions, or other unfavorable characteristics. Parcels of unused land may have been by-passed as the city expanded or they may have been cleared and subdivided prematurely in anticipation of future use which may or may not occur. It is evident that land use controls do not function as well as desired when such a large portion of urban land is unused.

The Planning Function

Although city planning is as old as cities, modern American city planning is conceded by many to have originated in Chicago with the Columbian Exposition of 1893.

The Chicago exposition was specifically intended to set a standard for architectural and urban design. The "Great White City" was built to the prevailing style of the period; Beaux Arts. The Beaux Arts style sought to design and place buildings to blend artfully with the environment.

The Great White City, was a design marvel of its time. Its courts, monumental buildings, curving walkways, lagoons, flowers, and woods, all in a curvilinear land use plan was a jewel of beauty and delight.

The Midway Plaisance was a parkway one mile long by one block wide abutting the Great White City. Commercial establishments were permitted only on the Midway. Buildings on the Midway were constructed to reflect their uses or to portray distinctive cultures. Pogodas, coffee pots, and Indian villages mingled with Dutch Windmills, Greek temples, and bean pots. The buildings were but plaster on lath but looked authentic. On the other hand, the Exposition proper was characterized by harmonious and authetically pleasing relationships among the many buildings and landscape features.

The impact of both White City and the Midway were tremendous. The one sparked the "City Beautiful" movement which resulted in the parks, civic centers, greenbelts, and walkways that enhanced many American cities. The other sparked the strip commercial districts which resulted in the (words of Tom Wolf) "Ring of ghastliness that surrounds each American city like the rind of some decaying fruit."

Daniel Burnham and Edward Bennett, architects of the Great White City of Chicago, followed that triumph by preparing a city plan for Chicago in 1909. The first modern national city planning conference was held in the same year.

Planning has significantly changed since then. Increasingly, professional planners conduct research and are concerned with administrative policy. They, in theory, are not decision makers, but recommend to clients and their employers alternative ways of reaching goals. They interpret community desires, and relative feasibilities of alternative solutions to problems. Further, information and advice from the Planning Department is often the only information and advice available that is based on systematic research. All this tends to make planners "VIP's" even though they make few if any actual decisions.

The functions of the planning department are to describe the city as it is and plan for its future. The Planner attacks these tasks through the use of air photos and maps (especially the land use map), through census data and state employment security data, through planning reports from the Federal government and other cities, and through field observation and questionnaire surveys. The planning products are reports, studies, information and recommendations.

SELECTED READINGS

Babcock, Richard, *The Zoning Game,* Madison, University of Wisconsin Press (1966).

Babcock, Richard F., *Billboards, Glass Houses and the Law,* Colorado Springs, Colorado, Shepard's Inc. (1977).

Chapin, F. Stuart, Jr., *Urban Land Use Planning,* Urbana: University of Illinois Press, 2nd edit., (1965).

Clauson, Marion, "Urban Land", Chapter 3 of: Marion Clauson, *America's Land and Its Uses.* Baltimore, published for Resources for the Future, Inc., by the Johns Hopkins University Press, (1972), pp. 30-56.

Griffith, Daniel A., "Evaluating the Transformation From a Monocentric to a Polycentric City," *Professional Geographer,* Vol. 33, No. 2 (May 1981) pp. 189-196.

Hagman, Donald G., "A New Deal: Trading Windfalls for Wipeouts," *Planing,* Vol. 40, No. 8 (Sept. 1974) pp. 9-13.

Lewis, Pierce F., Lownthal, David and Tuan, Yi-Fu, *Visual Blight in America,* Washington, D.C., The Association of the American Geographers, Resource Paper No. 23 (1973).

Manvel, Allen D., "Land Use in 106 Large Cities", in: *Three Land Research Studies,* prepared for the consideration of the National Commission on Urban Problems, Research Report No. 12. Washington: US Government Printing Office, (1968), pp. 19-60.

Mayer, Harold M., "Geography in City and Regional Planning", in: John W. Frazier (editor), *Applied Geography: Selected Perspectives.* Englewood Cliffs, N.J.: Prentice-Hall, Inc., (1982), pp. 25-57.

O'Keefe, Phil and Halverson, Bret, "If We Live in Cities, Let's Learn About Them," *Journal of Geography,* Vol. 79, No. 3 (March 1980) pp. 100-104.

Panel on Land Use Planning, *Land Use Planning,* Washington, D.C., National Academy of Sciences (1975).

Rubin, Barbara, "Aesthetic Ideology and Urban Design," *Annals of the Association of American Geographers,* Vol. 69, No. 3 (1979) pp. 339-361.

Scott, Mel, *American City Planning Since 1890*. Berkeley and Los Angeles; University of California Press, (1969).

So, Frank S., et. al. (editors), *The Practice of Local Government Planning*. Washington: International City Management Association, (1979).

Walker, Richard A. and Heiman, Michael K., "Quiet Revolution for Whom?" *Annals of The Association of American Geographers*, Vol. 71, No. 1, (March 1981) pp. 67-83.

Watson, J. Wreford, "Image Geography: The Myth of America in the American Scene," *The Advancement of Science*, Vol. 27 (1970-71) pp. 1-9.

Weaver, Clifford L. and Babcock, Richard F., "City Zoning the Once and Future Frontier," *Planning*, Vol. 45 No. 12 (Dec. 1979) pp. 19-23.

Weber, Max, *The City*, New York, Free Press (1958).

CHAPTER FOUR

The Land Within the City: Urban Sites

Geographers refer to urban location at two scales: **situation** and **site**. *Situation* refers to the location of the city relative to the area external to that city, and with which it interacts in numerous ways: its *hinterland* or *umland*, literally, the land behind or around the city. *Site,* on the other hand, refers to the conditions within the area occupied by the city. Site conditions have great influence upon the character of a city and upon its spatial form. Although many modifications can be made to sites, they are expensive, and planners must be greatly concerned with conditions of slope, drainage, soils, underlying rock, local climate, and the existence of local natural site hazards.

Site conditions may facilitate the development and growth of cities in accordance with desirable spatial patterns, or they may inhibit or prevent certain developments. In the words of Ian McHarg, it is easier to "design with nature" than to combat it.

Urban land derives its value primarily as a result of accessibility which, in turn, is related to the configurations of the transportation systems. The transportation routes are in most instances conditioned by local conditions of slope, drainage, foundation conditions, and other natural attributes which influence gradients, curvature, cuts and fills, bridges and tunnels, and circuity.

We will consider urban sites from three viewpoints: (1) terrain, or the surface configuration of the land, (2) local weather and climate, and (3) natural hazards associated with sites.

Terrain

Cities tend to be associated with relatively level land surfaces. Streets, railroad lines, utility lines, and boundaries of properties, as well as the design and construction of buildings are easiest where the land is level. On the other hand, if the land is too flat, drainage problems may have to be treated, resulting in additional costs.

Slopes — Very gentle slopes produce some advantages for city development, as contrasted to the total absence of slope, but in most instances steep slopes are a disadvantage. Steep slopes commonly produce rapid runoff of storm waters. This may result in the need for measures to mitigate soil erosion and the undermining of rocks along and behind the slopes. Steep slopes and bluffs along shorelines of rivers, lakes and oceans may be especially vulnerable to erosion and undermining, and it is not uncommon for buildings along the shore bluffs to be undermined, resulting in total loss. Although sites on and atop bluffs located at the outside of river meanders may offer scenic outlooks — and in earlier times defensive advantages — they are especially vulnerable to undermining, and may require very elaborate and expensive revetment works to inhibit the erosion.

If the underlying material of sites on or immediately above bluffs or steep slopes is soft and unconsolidated, the sites are especially vulnerable. In the hills north of Los Angeles, and along the Pacific shore west and northwest of the city, for example, very expensive homes were — and still continue to be — constructed on terraces molded from the hillsides. Since the hills are composed of soft materials, and because during the winter rainy season the torrents race down narrow canyons created by headward erosion of the numerous small and intermittent streams, the homes are periodically threatened as their sites are obliterated by mudslides. Added to the erosion hazard in such situations is the danger of brush fire during the summer dry seasons. Many expensive homes, in many metropolitan areas but especially in the southwestern United States, have been lost as a result of one or the other of these hazards, affecting, alternately, the same sites.

By clearance of vegetation from the vicinities of these sites, the danger of erosion is increased; in reducing one hazard another is thus increased.

Another disadvantage of urban development on slopes, and especially steep slopes, is the increased difficulty and cost of providing utility services, such as water lines and sewer outfalls, as compared with the costs of such facilities on relatively level land. These additional costs commonly mean that sites on hill slopes, or on the uplands above them, can be occupied only by the more expensive homes, and hence there may be a vertical altitudinal stratification of socio-economic groups, with the wealthy and upper-middle-class residential developments at higher elevations, and the poorer housing located in valleys between the upland surfaces. This stratification is prominent in such locations as that of Pittsburgh, where the better residential areas are on the Alleghany Plateau surfaces and the poorer residential areas in proximity to industrial areas in the valleys, where rivers and major highways as well as railroads favor "water level" routes, with minimal gradients. The local climatic conditions, too, in such locations vary vertically; the valley fogs, together with industry-caused air pollution make valley locations especially undesirable for housing.

In some areas, the vertical socio-economic stratification is just the opposite of that noted above: the poorer residential areas are at the higher elevations and on the slopes, with the better housing on the lowlands. This is especially true in many of the "third world" cities, such as in Latin America, where the prestigeous central locations are in the lower areas, while the costs of providing utility services to the slope and upland areas discourage them completely, so that unprovided with public water supplies and sewerage facilities, the hills and slopes tend to be occupied by the poorest housing, commonly without legal title to the sites.

Slopes also affect the costs, and hence availability, of transportation. In order to avoid slopes — to minimize gradients — railroads and roads may be very circuitous, thus spreading out the gradient over distances many times longer than the most direct one. Alternatives may be cuts and fills, tunnels, and bridges. In some cities, steep slopes, where the gradients of roads and railroads which depend upon adhesion would be impossibly great, inclines — variously called funiculars, inclined railways, or cableways — may be used. Suspended vehicles with overhead cables are also common; these are sometimes called "teleferiques", the most familiar form of which in the United States is the ski lift. Cable cars, attached to continuous underground cables in the street beds, were common in cities throughout the world during the late nineteenth and early twentieth centuries and they remain as familiar tourist attractions and as parts of the local transit network in San Francisco where they were originally developed a century earlier.

Although slopes and hills present many disadvantages, they also may be advantageous. If they were not, high class residential developments would not have taken place on such sites. Hills and slopes offer opportunities to take advantage of the scenery in capitalizing on prime sites with interesting outlooks. To protect such sites against undesirable encroachments into the sight lines various legal restrictions may be invoked, such as scenic easements, which in some instances may involve payment to the owners of the intervening properties in return for restricting them from building into the restricted airspace.

Unfortunately, many otherwise scenic sites have had their potentialities destroyed by the imposition of street patterns which prevent the maximum scenic possibilities from being realized. When, for example, a rectangular grid-iron pattern of streets is superimposed upon an irregular terrain, outlooks of unique scenic interest may be less evident, or may be destroyed altogether. A rigid street pattern on irregular terrain often produces the additional disadvantage, as in San Francisco, Seattle, and other cities, of street gradients which make vehicular operation, or even pedestrian movements, difficult or impossible, while at the same time exascerbating the difficulties of drainage and increasing the possibilities of erosion and landslides.

Other site conditions involving hazardous slopes include these located in valleys below dams and reservoirs, where overflows, or even dam failures, may produce catastrophies; the rush of water through the narrow valleys may be very sudden. There have also been many catastrophies resulting from the positioning of mine wastes above developed valley areas.

Geologists and engineers recognize an "angle of repose" for each type of material, whether the slope is natural or artificial. When the angle of repose is exceeded, whether because of undermining, seepage of water behind the slope, or pressure behind a dam or a spoil bank of mined material, the potential for catastrophy is great. Similarly, in mountainous areas, urban development may be threatened by rock falls and by avalanches.

Bedrock and foundation conditions — The underlying materials vitally affect the feasibility and costs of urban development. Unstable foundation conditions must be avoided, and structures must be designed and built in a manner to assure that they will not sink into the ground, be undermined, or tilt. The Leaning Tower of Pisa, of course, is the classic example of the latter instance, but there are many buildings in most cities which are more-or-less "out of plumb" because of irregular or unstable foundation conditions. Building collapses due to such conditions are not uncommon. In the older portions of some cities, the sidewalks have a noticeable tilt toward the roadway and away from the building line, in anticipation of the slow sinking of the building, which, it was anticipated, would eventually produce a more level sidewalk. Modern engineering has made such empirical guesswork less common, but buildings may still sink slowly under certain conditions.

Many buildings rest on piles, driven into the ground, with the entire weight of the building resting on piles, located under the vertical members of the structures themselves, the weight being transferred to the columns above the piles by horizontal structural members. The steel-frame skyscraper, first developed in the 1880s, utilizes this principle. The cost of a structure is greatly affected, of course, by the number and depth of the piles which are required. These are, in turn, a function of the character and depth of the horizontal conditions and depth of either the bedrock or of hard supporting formations above the bedrock. Until a few years ago, it was not considered possible to erect tall buildings in such cities as New Orleans, where the soft and relatively unconsolidated underground material, brought down and deposited during floods of the Mississippi River could not support heavy weights, and where the distance to bedrock would have made piles economically unfeasible. Generally, sites on deltas, such as that of the Mississippi, were disadvantageous for urban development, for many reasons, although the situation, in such instances, at or near the mouth of a river system draining a large and productive hinterland, may be sufficiently advantageous as to compensate for the poor site conditions.

In order to overcome the limitations of great depth to bedrock, or of unstable foundation conditions extending down for considerable distances, spreading the weight of the building over larger areas than those involving just pilings may be advantageous. Spread footings, in which the weight of the pilings is spread horizontally, may be used. For very large and tall buildings, the footings may actually coalesce horizontally, so that the weight of the building is spread over the entire ground area covered by the structure, or even greater area. In such instances, the building may actually "float" on the soft underlying material, in much the same manner as a raft floats on water. Care needs to be taken of course, that the weight of the structure is evenly distributed, otherwise tilting or even collapse may occur. Lighter and smaller structures, such as residences, may rest on slabs of concrete or other materials not penetrating far below the surface of the ground; the floating principle is the same. In such instances, the buildings do not have basements. On many sites a high water-table would make provision of basements difficult in any event.

A contrasting site condition is where hard rock outcrops are located close to the land surface, where it is necessary to excavate for basements by blasting. One may wonder, for example, how the weight of the many tall skyscrapers in Manhattan is supported. Part of the answer is that the hard pre-Cambrian chrystalin rock which is close to the surface and which outcrops in many parts of the island furnishes firm support, but an additional consideration is that in many instances the weight of material excavated for the basement may actually be greater than the weight of the building, so that the total weight to be supported after the building is constructed is actually less than before.

Building materials — The rock and other materials associated with urban sites may have such characteristics that they furnish prospective or actual materials for building and other purposes. Planners have been known, in many instances, to overlook the fact that the sites proposed for buildings and other developments may contain the very materials which are needed for construction within the city, or, on the other hand, constitute valuable resources which could be transported elsewhere and thus contribute substantially to the economic base of the city. In such instances, it should be determined whether the economic and other advantages of exploiting the materials would outweigh the advantages of normal urban development of the same sites, or whether the environmental impacts of extracting the materials would adversely affect other sites in the vicinity to the extent of being incompatible. Where the sites are owned by private interests, which expect to extract the materials, negotiations between the public agencies and the owners must be conducted if the conflicts are to be resolved.

In some instances, mining of the underground materials meant that the prior urban developments on the surface had to be terminated and the structures removed. There have been instances where entire towns and cities were re-located to provide access to the underground resources. A notable example is Hibbing, Minnesota, which was originally built atop a rich deposit of iron ore. When the nearby open pit mine, which eventually became the largest such operation in the world and the most prolific source of hematite, reached the point at which expansion to the site of the city was desired, the entire city was removed to another site. When the mining community is a company town, of course, the relocation may be easier. Another example is Bingham, Utah, which was located along the line of expansion of what is generally claimed to be the world's largest open pit copper mine; when the company decided to mine close to the town, the entire community closed down and was removed.

Subsidence is a man-made hazard when underground mining is carried on. Both in the location and the development of the community on the one hand and in the design and operation of the mines on the other, the possibility of subsidence must be considered. Extensive subsidence of Scranton, Pennsylvania, took place as the result of anthracite mining under the city. Large portions of Long Beach, California, subsided more than thirty feet as oil was extracted from underneath the city, and it was necessary to build bulkheads to prevent the ocean from inundating the lowered portions of the city, while streets and highways had to be put on high embankments to avoid closure as they slowly sank below the sea level. On the other hand, the Port of Long Beach benefitted, not only from the revenues from the oil taxes, which legally had to be used for the port, but also from the fact that the extraction of the oil and the consequent subsidence of the harbor bottom made dredging unnecessary.

Building materials are typically bulky, and of relatively low value in proportion to their bulk and weight. Therefore, they cannot usually stand long-distance transportation, unless both the origins and the destinations are located where direct water transportation is available. Where suitable clay is available near a city, brickyards need to be provided, insofar as they are not incompatible with other urban development. Limestone, used not only as a building stone, but also as the principal ingredient in cement, and as ballast for roads and railroads, is a natural resource needed in city building. In developing a land-use plan for a city or metropolitan area, sites for the extraction and processing of such resources must be considered, and decisions must be made as to whether the advantages of local availability and processing, and consequently low transportation costs, outweigh the advantages of alternate uses for the sites.

Similarly, biotic resources useful in construction, where they occur near cities, raise the problem of the relative advantages and disadvantages of their exploitation. Wood is, of course, still a basic building material, and the proximity of forests to some cities may be an advantage in lowering building costs, providing, of course that the trees, being generally a scarce resource, are to be eventually replaced, either at the same site, or elsewhere. Where the local forest resources are to be utilized, the city or metropolitan plan should consider possible sites for lumber mills, pulp mills, and, in some instances, paper mills. Because these are "heavy" industries, the environmental impacts upon local air and water conditions must be given serious consideration.

Shorelines — Urban sites adjacent to bodies of water — the oceans, lakes, and rivers — are generally advantageous, but such sites present a set of conditions which vitally affect the spatial patterns of land use, existing and prospective, within the urban area, and there commonly are natural hazards along and beyond the land-water contact.

Shore frontage is a scarce resource, and many alternative land uses compete for shore locations. As for most urban land uses, the competition drives prices up, and those uses which can most effectively pay the price win out. Because the public interest may not always coincide with the "highest and best use" of the scarce shore land, it is very often necessary that regulations and special restrictions be imposed upon lands bordering the water. These regulations and restrictions take a number of forms, including zoning, environmental controls, and, in some states, special restrictions under the category of "coastal zone management" (CZM).

Of special concern are the regulations concerning the use of the waters. In the eastern United States, the governing principle is that of riperian rights, in which the properties bordering the surface water bodies have the right to use the water without restriction, other than those relating to environmental quality. In most of the western states title to the land does not include the right to use either the surface water adjoining the property, or even located on the property, nor does ownership of the land include the right to use the underground waters. There, the water rights are in terms of prior appropriation, or "first come first served", since the quantity of water is commonly less than the demand for it. Water rights in such states are saleable commodities, just as the land is subject to transfer of ownership by sale. Cooperative organizations, as well as special purpose governmental districts, may be formed to control and regulate the use of water. Some of the agencies created for the purpose are very large governmental units, as, for example, those serving metropolitan Los Angeles, which must get its water by means of complex reservoir and aquaduct systems from the distant Colorado River and from northern California. In many instances, the prospective or actual uses of the land for urban purposes must compete directly with the demand for water by agriculture. Comprehensive plans must be made and implemented for multiple use of the scarce water resources, and the water scarcity may impose limits upon the extent of urban growth.

Regardless of the availability — or lack of availability — of water as an essential commodity, locations adjacent to shorelines tend to be subject to intense competition.

There are some urban land uses which *must* be located on shores, either because of the need for direct contact with the water bodies, or because they consume or utilize large quantities of water. In the former category are port terminals and port-associated industries, shipyards, and marinas for recreational boating. In the latter are electric generating plants, which use water for cooling, iron and steel plants, cement plants, oil refineries, and other "heavy" industries which use water not only for cooling, but also may utilize low-cost water transportation for the receipt of raw materials and the shipment of products. Also, some large industries benefit from proximity to large bodies of water for disposal of their waste materials, buth liquid and solid. Environmental controls, especially since the passage of the EPA act in 1969, have been increasingly initiated and, to a greater or lesser degree, enforced, with regard to the disposal of wastes. Treatment of waste waters before they are discharged is generally mandatory, although the extent of the treatment may be controversial. Sewerage treatment and disposal plants are advantageously located adjacent to water bodies, not only to utilize the water in the treatment process, but also to dispose of the effluent into the water bodies, after treatment. Similarly, if municipal or industrial water supplies are to be derived from bodies of surface water, the intakes and treatment plants derive advantage from locations as close as possible to the water sources.

Parks constitute major uses of water frontage and land adjacent to water bodies in many cities and metropolitan areas. Water-based recreational activities are important, not only in supplying inherent needs of the population for such activities, but also in constituting major elements of the urban and metropolitan economic base. Supplying facilities and services for recreational boating, for sport fishing, water skiing and other forms of water-based recreation constitute important inputs to the local economies in many areas. The scenic aspects of shorelines are also significant, and the creation and maintenance of parks may contribute heavily to the maintenance of the scenic amenities.

Beaches, of course, are major uses of many shorelines, and they, too, constitute significant sources of local income. On the other hand, over-use of some beaches may tend to reduce the amenity values, the very ones which people seek. Public control over the land uses adjacent to the beaches must, in most instances, constitute important elements of the land-use plans for communities, cities ad metropolitan areas. Many beach areas are included in city, county, regional, state ad national parks; some are world-famous. The U.S. National Park Service has control over a significant number of beaches, in conformance with the relatively new emphasis of the federal government in emphasizing market-oriented locations along with the traditional policy of resource-orientation; that is, ccreation and maintenance of national recreational facilities where they are accessible to urban populations. Notable examples are the recreational shoreline on a portion of Cape Cod, the National Recreational park embracing portions of the bay and ocean shorelines within New York City and nearby areas in New York and New Jersey, the Indiana Dunes National Lakeshore in northwestern Indiana close to the Chicago-Gary complex, and the Cuyahoga Valley National Recreational area between Cleveland and Akron, Ohio, which not only preserves an invaluable scenic area but also provides recreation, under controlled conditions, accessible to several nearby metropolitan areas, large and small.

In several of these instances, public ownership and direct control was secured only after long battles with private interests. In the instance of the Indiana Dunes, for example, the conservationists and recreational-oriiented interests fought vigorously the plans to place a large iron and steel plant and a major port in the vicinity.. After years of conflict, mutual accommodation was achieved, and the National Lakeshore was achieved as well as the industrial plant and port. Although there is some degree of impingement upon the scenic aspect of the public reservation, it is minimal.

Public access to shorelines is a significant problem in some areas. Riparian ownership of much shoreline restricts or prevents public access in many areas, and in some instances the riparian rights must be purchased by public agencies in order to make the beaches and waterfronts available to the public. In some cities, the only direct public access is at the ends of public streets. Uninterrupted public access along some stretches of shoreline is secured by laws — in a few instances at the state level — requiring riparian owners to maintain an access route paralleling the shore across their properties. Objections to this procedure are often raised on the grounds that such access reduces the security on the individual properties.

The maintenance of beaches and the protection of both public and private properties along shorelines against the dangers of erosion is a constant battle. Shorelines, by their nature, tend to be unstable. The flows of rivers, and littoral currents in the oceans, bays, and large lakes, constantly remove materials along the shores and deposit them elsewhere. Many ports maintain access only as the result of constant or intermittent dredging of their access channels and the dredging of materials alongside the terminals. Lakes behind dams eventually silt and depths must be maintained by dredging. On the other hand, beaches may be removed as the shore currents erode them, while depositing materials further along the shore where they may not be desired.

Shore protection, therefore, is an important consideration, and it may involve substabtial expenditures of public funds. Riparian private owners of shoreline properties commonly cannot afford the great costs of protecting their own properties. Very often whatever efforts are made by such owners, the scale would be insufficient to provide the desired protection, and some form of cooperative or public action may be deeded. A conspicuous example of thelarge-scale effort which may be deeded is at Miami Beach, Florida, where sandy beach was removed by action of winds, waves, and littoral currents through the years, to the extent that only very small stretches of sand were available, mainly on the sides of groins, or bulkheads at right angles to the shore, where the sand-laden waters could be intercepted. But the beaches were so narrowed that not only was there very limited public access, but the many hotels and apartment buildings along the beach had to install very expensive "sea walls" to protect the properties and the structures on them from erosion and undermining. The federal government had to supply vast quantities of sand to replace the beach which in the course of the years had been eroded away. There is little doubt that, if the present artificial beach is to be retained, the process will have to be repeated in the future.

Local Urban Weather and Climate

Within urban areas, the character and spatial arrangement of land uses and structures exert significant impacts upon the local weather and climate.

"Heat Island" — The air over cities tends generally to be warmer than the air over the nearby countryside. This gives rise to what is called the "heat island". Maps of temperature at any given time usually show isotherms (contours connecting points of equal temperature) arranged in a generally concentric pattern, with the highest temperatures recorded at the center of the city, or where the density of buildings and pavements is greatest. Paving materials, whether on the ground or on roofs, absorb and store heat energy during the daytime hours and radiate it slowly during the nights. The relative absence of vegetation in the densely-built urban areas also contributes to the heat island by increasing the amount of heat which is absorbed.

The differential heating of the built-up urban areas also influences air circulation and wind patterns. The heat of the city causes the air to rise, and the replacement of the air is responsible for movement of the cooler air from the nearby non-urban areas to reach the city. Thus a local circulation pattern is established, with the outward flow of air at higher elevations and the inward flow closer to the ground. Where the flow is constrained or confined, local turbulence commonly occurs. Tall buildings may focus the air in the relatively confined areas between them, causing a "wind tunnel" effect. Air travelers are often well aware of the turbulance over the cities, especially at low altitudes.

Surface Irregularity — Not only does the presence of buildings create air turbulence by interfering with and confining the horizontal air flow, but the walls of the buildings absorb solar energy, especially during the early and late times of the day when the sun is at a low angle. This contributes to the heat island by increasing the absorbtion of solar energy, while at the same time changing the local air circulation pattern.

Evaporation and Transpiration — Contributing to the increased temperature is built-up areas of cities are the relative absence of vegetative ground cover and trees, and the effects of buildings and pavement on run -off of water. Precipitation runs off more rapidly under such circumstances; hence evaporation is reduced, and the heat energy that would have been used in the process of evaporation is absorbed. The lesser transpiration due to scarcity of vegetation has the same effect; the reduction of both processes thus tends to increase the temperature of the urban areas.

Generation of Heat — Industrial processes and space heating as well as transportation use fossil fuels, the burning of which produces heat, much of which escapes into the atmosphere. In cities, of course, this heat, which is essentially wasted energy, escapes into the atmosphere, thereby raising the air temperature, which, in turn, tends to intensify the air circulation patterns noted above.

The presence of people in the high-density portions of cities also may have a noticeable effect in raising the air temperature.

Air Pollution — Anyone who has flown over a city in daylight is aware of the fact that the visibility is less than in the non-urban areas. Typically, one observes a dome-shaped area of air pollution, with the pollution extending for a considerable distance along the down-wind direction from the concentrated urban-industrial area.

Particulate matter — smoke and dust — obviously tends to be greater over and near cities than in the surrounding non-urban areas. These particulates reflect solar radiation, thereby decreasing insolation, and thus somewhat compensating for the heating effects noted above. On the other hand, the clouds over cities, in part caused or intensified by the particulate matter, gives rise to a "greenhouse effect", especially if local conditions prevent rapid movement of the air. This effect consists of trapping of the heat generated as a result of urban structures, pavements and activities.

Urban areas tend to have greater cloudiness, rain and snow, than nearby non-urban areas, except, in many instances, those located downwind from the city, where the winds carry the moisture away from the city. Particulates form condensation nucleii for the moisture in the air, causing fogs and precipitation.

There is also some evidence that the contrails from numerous aircraft flying at certain altitudes in the vicinities of large cities which are major air transportation hubs form cirrus clouds which reduce the solar energy reaching the ground, and thus, to some extent, modify the local climate.

The trapping of warmer air over cities, especially where local terrain and other conditions give rise to temperature inversions, often may trap the pollutants. Not only do the activities in the central parts of the cities tend to get trapped under the inversion layers, but the particulates and the gases generated by industrial activities on the fringes of the cities and beyond may be transported into the central portions of the urban areas by the air circulation patterns that are the results of the central-area heating effects previously noted, in which the heat island effect is evidenced in part by the movement of air at low altitudes toward the urban center, where replacement takes place of the air which rises as a result of the heating of the central portions of the urban area. Industrial activities plus the exhausts from thousands of motor vehicles together may cause illnesses and even deaths from the concentrations of polluted air. The "smog", as in Los Angeles, may be intensified by the inversion layers, especially where local terrain inhibits or prevents free circulation of the air trapped within the inversion. Cities such as Los Angeles, where hills or mountains interfere with circulation, are especially vulnerable. Mexico City is noted for its smogs, and where industrial activities in valleys cause pollution which is trapped by temperature inversions, as in the industrial valleys of western Pennsylvania, health conditions may be seriously affected.

Carbon monoxide is especially prevalent in the air over urban areas. It is predominantly caused by the concentrations of motor vehicles, and in heavy concentrations it is lethal. Nitrogen oxides, also the result of motor vehicle operation, reacts with oxygen to form nitrogen dioxide, which has adverse effects on biological processes. Sunlight acts upon nitrogen dioxide to create photochemical smog.

Natural Hazards

No place is completely free from natural hazards. The presence of particular types of hazards, and the degree of vulnerability to them however, vary widely from place to place. Since people and facilities are concentrated in urban areas, such areas are especially vulnerable to interference to normal activities, loss or damage to property, and injury and loss of life. Human adjustments to the natural hazards may range from disregard of them, to avoidance, prevention, and compensation. Not all hazards lend themselves to each of these kinds of adjustments. Geographers and planners, during the most recent two or three decades, have become increasingly aware of the consequences of hazards in urban areas, and are gradually developing some knowledge of how to cope with them.

Some hazards are more or less persistent, and are constantly or frequently present in some regions and places; others are infrequent and may be catastrophic.

Examples of hazards which are constant or frequent are often associated with climate. Heating of interior spaces in winter, and, more recently, cooling in summer, are, of course, familiar types of adjustments. Humidification and dehumidification are also increasingly common. In many cities, enclosed spaces extend beyond individual buildings in the forms of subterranean pedestrian and shopping areas, roofs over streets; and upper-level walkways with pedestrian bridges, enclosed, over streets, are increasingly familiar in the high-density areas of many cities where extremes of temperature, rain, snow, or high winds would otherwise make outdoor activities uncomfortable, or from time to time impossible. In some central business districts, as in Montreal, Philadelphia, Minneapolis, St. Paul, and Milwaukee, such climate-protected interior spaces may extend for many blocks, or even for miles. Among the earliest of such inter-connected continuous enclosed activity spaces was the Grand Central Terminal district in mid-Manhattan, where many buildings were — and are — interconnected.

Among the catastrophic hazards are floods, tornadoes, hurricanes, earthquakes, volcanic eruptions, tsunami, landslides, avalanches, subsidence, heavy snows and icing conditions, and many others. A few of these phenomena occur with frequency; others are rare and unpredictable.

Floods — Floods are among the natural hazards which have been subjected to considerable investigation, and to which adjustments can increasingly be made. Geographers, in particular, have been active in flood research, and, at least, in part the result of their investigations of urban floods, a number of public policies have been initiated to deal with flood problems.

There are two basic ways of adjusting to the flood hazard. One is to try to keep the floods away from people and buildings; the other is to keep people and buildings away from the areas subject to floods.

Floods are predictable. The flood-prone areas can be readily identified and their boundaries determined broadly, within the present state of knowledge. Within flood-prone areas, the flood frequencies and degree of risk can be determined. It remains to complete and to continuously up-date the surveys which are required to assess the probable extent and degree of flood risk. With this knowledge it is possible to guide private decisions and public policies to deal with the risks.

By definition, any location within a flood plain will, sooner or later, be flooded. If investments are to be made in buildings, roads, railroads and other facilities in flood plains, they must be made with knowledge of the risks, and with arrangements to minimize loss and damage, or to compensate in some way for the prospective loss and damage. As a result of extensive flood research, largely by geographers, the U.S. Geological Survey, with the cooperation of state and local governments, has been conducting a series of flood hazard mapping surveys, in which the flood-prone areas of the nation are being identified on large-scale maps. Financing of investments in flood-prone areas which are so identified cannot generally be arranged unless the investments are covered by flood insurance. In most instances, the design of buildings in flood plains must take into consideration certain provisions which minimize the danger of damage from floods.

Flood plains attract many urban land uses. Rivers furnish low-cost transportation, especially for bulk materials, including fossil fuels, ores, grain, and other commodities which, in turn attract industrial establishments which receive or ship such materials by water. Until the 1980s improvements and maintenance of the navigable channels used in interstate commerce within the United States was free of charges against the users, but in the early 1980s a system of user charges was initiated, which may somewhat mitigate the supposed competitive advantages of large-scale bulk transportation by water over other modes of transportation. Many of the large-scale projects for improvement and management of the rivers are multiple-purpose projects and programs, and in some instances it is difficult to determine the proportions of the costs which are attributable to navigation.

Many of the river improvement projects not only are intended to benefit or facilitate navigation, but also are designed as flood-control projects. River regulation by dams, commonly circumvented by navigation locks, are common. Levees are designed to prevent streams from overflowing their banks, and, in urban areas, levees and flood walls are intended to prevent inundations of the occupied areas during high flood stages. Groins or piers extending into the streams confine the waters to narrower but deeper channels, and the scouring action of the currents then deepens the channels, thus more effectively handling the greater volumes of water during floods.

It has been demonstrated that such engineering works may reduce or even eliminate, the damage potential from small and medium floods, but there is no assurance that meteorological and hydrological conditions may not, at some future time, create a flood which exceeds the design capacity of such engineering constructions. In such an event, the results may be catastrophic; much more intense than if the construction of the flood-control works had not occurred. One study indicated that the actual damage, over the years, from such catastrophic floods, calculated on an average annual basis, exceeded the damage that would have resulted from lack of such "protection", if all floods had been permitted to cover the land which would have been vulnerable without such works. The reason is that the availability of flood-protection works gives a false sense of security, and tends to encourage investment and construction in flood-prone areas, thereby increasing the damage potential from the rare but extreme flood.

Generally, flood-prone urban areas can be divided into two categories. One is the "floodway" where *any* construction should be prohibited; this is the area along the streams where frequent floods occur. The other area is that which would be inundated by a "hundred year" flood, that is, a flood with an expected frequency of once in a century. In such areas, construction is generally permitted, provided that it is of flood-resistant character, and that insurance against flood damage is prerequisite to the securing of finance for the intended construction.

There are several types of urban land use which are appropriate for flood plains, and which serve the purpose of discouraging intensive use and investment in the flood-prone area.

In floodways, construction can be prevented by local zoning, which would permit only low-density uses, preferably those which do not include permanent buildings. In many instances, property owners may demand compensation for the restriction of the use of their property. A more effective method is for public purchase of the land areas included in the floodways along the stream banks, and the subsequent use of the land adjacent to the stream courses for low-density public uses such as parks, forest preserves, golf courses, and — in certain circumstances where they would not interfere with the stream flow or be incompatible with nearby uses — sanitary landfill. The use of floodways and adjacent flood-prone lands as park and forest preserve not only serves the purpose of preventing investment and possible heavy financial loss from floods, but also facilitates public policy implementation in providing land-use practices, with or without engineering works, intented to mitigate the flood crests. These include maintenance of wooded areas and soil conservation practices to retard runoff. At the same time, both passive and active recreation facilities can be provided in the public parks and wooded areas. County park and forest preserve districts in such metropolitan areas as Chicago, Milwaukee, and Cleveland utilize large extents of land bordering the rivers and creeks for these purposes.

Hurricane Coastal Flooding — A special circumstance of flood potential in some of the urbanized areas of the United States is that of the many barrier beaches and offshore islands, extending from New England to Texas along the coasts of the Atlantic Ocean and the Gulf of Mexico. These areas, including many resort communities and several large cities, are especially vulnerable to tropical hurricanes which form in the Atlantic and proceed generally in a westerly direction, sometimes curving up the Atlantic coast. As they proceed inland, they gradually weaken, but their damage potential continues, since they may cause valley flooding. Even more potentially catastrophic are the high water levels, accompanied by powerful waves and strong winds, which may completely inundate the low-lying coastal beaches, with force sufficient to destroy even the largest and best-constructed buildings. The problem is compounded by the fact that most such barrier beaches are comprised of sand which can be removed by the hurricane-associated waves and winds. Many such situations, including both the sandy barrier beaches and the coral reefs of the Florida keys, are the sites of dense urban development, connected to the mainland only by a few — frequently only one — bridge, with insufficient capacity to evacuate the population in the time available following a hurricane warning. Among the especially vulnerable urban areas are those on the south shore of Long Island, the resorts of New Jersey coast including Atlantic City and Ocean City, the many resort communities of the "outer banks" of North Carolina, the cities of the Atlantic coast of Florida, such as Palm Beach, Fort Lauderdale, Hollywood and Miami Beach, and several major cities of the Gulf Coast such as Galveston and Corpus Christi, Texas. Several such cities have experienced severe damage and loss of life in previous hurricanes, when their population, and hence loss potential, was much less than now.

Tsunami — Tsunami, incorrectly called "tidal waves", are closely related, in terms of their damage potential, to hurricane waves, although their cause is quite different, and they are not usually accompanied by strong winds. They are typically caused by earthquakes, which may be many thousands of miles — commonly on another continent — from the shores where they cause the damage. They cross the oceans rapidly, but in so doing are barely noticeable, until they reach a beach or shore, where they may suddenly rise scores of feet high. In some instances, tsunami have been observed to exceed a hundred feet in height. Tsunami-prone areas, like stream flood-prone areas, can be mapped, but with less assurance, as the maximum heights are uncertain. The

Honolulu telephone directory, for example, contains several pages of maps of the areas which would be evacuated, time permitting, in the event of a tsunami warning. Unlike other types of floods, however, tsunami are not entirely predictable; they may appear with little or no warning. In most circumstances, however, they are caused by distant earthquakes or volcanic eruptions, in distant coastal areas or under the ocean.

Earthquakes — Although some seismologists believe that the prediction of earthquakes may achieve some reliability in the near future, catastrophic earthquakes are still common in many areas, and few authorities would be willing to take the risk of a false prediction. Like floods, however, earthquake potential is unevenly distributed, and, although most areas may be subject to seismic activity, the areas of high earthquake vulnerability are generally well known. Such areas include some of the world's largest cities, a number of which have suffered disastrous earthquakes in the past. The most vulnerable areas in North America are along the "Pacific Rim", including the Aleutian Islands and the coast of Alaska, and especially the west coast of the contiguous United States. The San Francisco earthquake of 1906 is well-known, but the metropolitan area of Los Angeles is also extremely vulnerable. Architects in California, among other places, are required to, in order to secure a license to practice, to be knowledgeable about "earthquake resistant" construction. Building codes in many urban communities require certain structural measures to reduce earthquake vulnerability of structures. But, analogous to flood-protection measures, there is no complete assurance that earthquakes will not cause extreme damage and casualties. Unless earthquake forecasting can be developed far beyond present knowledge, there is no possibility of evacuation of the densely-populated urban areas with vulnerability to that type of natural hazard. Evacuation of the millions of residents of southern California, including metropolitan Los Angeles and San Diego, or of the San Francisco-Oakland bay area, is unthinkable.

Although the maximum earthquake potential within North America is along the Pacific coast, major earthquakes occurred in the nineteenth century in the Midwest in 1811, and in Charleston, South Carolina, in 1886. Minor earthquakes frequently occur in New England, although none have yet caused substantial damage in that region.

In areas known to be earthquake-prone, construction of buildings on land which is especially subject to displacement, unfortunately, is not uncommon. Local ordinances should make such construction subject to mandatory earthquake-resistant measures, and, as in areas subject or infrequent, but inevitable, flooding, compulsory insurance. Local communities should, in spite of probable objections from those having a vested interest in developing such areas, make readily available the geological maps which indicate the nature of the ground conditions which are especially vulnerable to earthquakes. In general, areas on and near fault lines should be completely avoided, and all those concerned with development or occupancy of landfill areas or other land areas consisting of relatively unconsolidated materials should be made well aware of the inherent hazards of such sites. In San Francisco in 1906 and in Tokyo in 1933 the maximum damage from the earthquakes, as distinguished from the earthquake-caused fires, was on such sites. In some instances, coastal areas subject to high earthquake risk are also areas where the dangers from tsunami, either originating locally or at considerable distance, are also very high.

Volcanic activity — People in the United States were suddenly made aware of the hazards of volcanic activity with the eruption of Mount St. Helens in Washington State on May 18, 1980. Before that, most Americans thought of volcanic hazards as associated with distant lands on other continents. Nevertheless, the Pacific northwest including northern California, Oregon, Washington and Alaska, as well as Hawaii, have many volcanoes, extinct, dormant, and active, and many evidences of violent volcanic activity in the past.

The volcanic hazard is not highly localized in the vicinities of the volcanoes, and cities hundreds of miles distant may be affected by volcanic activity. In general, regions of volcanic activity roughly coincide with those of earthquake activity, however.

Volcanic activity may take any or all of three forms. It may be associated with earthquakes, it may produce disastrous lava flows, and it may result in the emission of ash and poisonous gases.

Urban areas have been destroyed by each of these manifestations of volcanism. Pompeii, probably the most famous although by no means the largest or most disastrous victim of volcanism, was destroyed by ashfall while most of its residents were killed by the gases. St. Pierre in Martinique, lost 30,000 people by ashes and gases. Considerable destruction in Iceland was caused by the same manifestations. Hilo, Hawaii, was threatened by lava flows.

Material flowing from or ejected from volcanoes may cause floods and extensive damage, by blocking or constricting rivers, or causing rises in the water levels of rivers and lakes, in some instances at considerable distances from the erupting volcano. Mt. St. Helens' eruption in 1980 caused considerable disruption to transportation in much of the Pacific Northwest. Access to the Port of Portland and to other ports along the Columbia and Willamette rivers was blocked for a considerable time. Portland may have suffered permanent loss of some of its port traffic as a result, because diversion to other routes, once having taken place, may change the traffic patterns from then on.

Unlike earthquakes, volcanic eruptions typically do not take place suddenly; there is commonly ample time for evacuation of the areas likely to be affected. Since eruptions cannot be prevented, and the effects cannot easily if at all be constrained, evacuation is the only feasible course of action. It may save lives, but destruction of property cannot be prevented to any extent except by avoidance of areas vulnerable to the effects of prospective eruptions. In this context, it is important to realize that a dormant volcano is not an extinct one.

Tornadoes — Tornadoes are violent circular winds caused by steep temperature gradients, encompassing very limited areas — unlike hurricanes — and moving rapidly along a narrow path, where the destruction may be complete. They cannot be prevented, and the warning time is very short, usually too short to permit evacuation. There are few areas which are not vulnerable to a greater or lesser degree, but maps are available showing the tornado frequency in the past. Insofar as urban land use is concerned, the only important provision that can be made is to design major buildings with basement shelters of heavy construction, and to require all buildings to have secure foundations, especially in regions of maximum tornado vulnerability and frequency. Much of the damage and loss of life is associated with relatively lightly-constructed frame buildings, and especially mobile homes on insecure foundations. However the force of a tornado is so powerful that relatively few buildings in the typical city can resist damage.

Landslides and avalanches — Landslides may be due to a number of causes, but generally they are caused by undermining, the agent being water. Coastal erosion and erosion along streams is a common cause, when the currents remove material causing the normal angle of repose of the material above to be exceeded. Heavy rains and storm action may cause undercutting, and many houses and other structures have been undermined along shorelines, as mentioned earlier.

Seepage may cause undermining, regardless of proximity to a body of water. This is especially true where the underlying material is soft and relatively unconsolidated. In the hills north of Los Angeles, for example, expensive homes, sited on terraces within the narrow canyons, have been destroyed by slippage of the underlying soft earth during and following torrential rains, which are common there in winter.

Landslides are especially apt to occur when vegetation is thin or has been removed in the vicinity, or above a slope, thereby permitting rapid penetration of the precipitation into the ground. Providing adequate vegetative cover may, in many instances, reduce the hazards from landslides. Spoil banks associated with mining activities should be provided with vegetative cover as soon as possible, in order to eliminate, or reduce, the danger of erosion and slides.

Similarly, avalanches may occur when the angle of repose of snow or ice is exceeded, by differential melting or otherwise. Obviously, the best protection against landslides and avalanches is not to occupy, insofar as possible, the lands below the bluffs or snowfronts. Even the heaviest retaining walls may be inadequate.

Other natural hazards — There are many other natural hazards affecting urban sites, and hence requiring consideration in the planning and building of cities. Among them are brush and forest fires, heavy snowfalls, flooding due to snowmelt, icing conditions, lightning, and so forth. Space does not permit discussion of each of these, but, in common with those discussed, each can be to some extent reduced or mitigated by increasing people's perception of them, through the educational institutions, mass media, and in some instances by mandatory requirements, such as zoning of land uses, which would discourage development in areas of high vulnerability, or which would require information regarding known hazard locations to be provided to prospective developers or occupants, as well as to prospective investors in properties located in hazardous areas.

Environmental perception — Geographers, planners, psychologists and others in recent years have been conducting research on how people perceive their environments, and how their environmental perceptions condition their actions and reactions, both to long-term hazards and to prospective and actual catastrophic events. Commonly, risks are either overlooked or dismissed. Houses on floodplains may be soon replaced on the same sites as those destroyed by a flood, eroded terraces may be reconstructed, wastes may be deposited in streams despite legal restrictions, thereby decreasing the available channels for movement of the water and increasing the flood danger. In general urban land uses must be planned and developed with greater cognizance of the site hazards than has commonly been the case.

Conclusion

An urban community, whether a neighborhood, city, or metropolitan area, is comprised of thousands of individual parcels of land, each of which is characterized by one or more uses. Although one may generalize about the site of such a community, the fact remains that each individual parcel, and hence each land use, is unique. The conventional models of urban structure and growth, the geometric and mathematical models — which, admittedly have some predictive value — cannot be used without the realization that no two communities have identical spatial patterns of land use, and that the anomolies due to special conditions of individual sites and groups of sites within the community must be taken into consideration.

SELECTED READINGS

Berry, Brian J. L. and Horton, Frank E., *Urban Environmental Management,* Englewood Cliffs, N.J., Prentice-Hall (1974).

Burton, Ian, Kates, Robert W., and White, Gilbert F., *The Environment as Hazard.* New York, Oxford University Press, (1978), 240 pp.

Changnon, Stanley A., Jr., "What to Do About Urban-Generated Weather and Climate Changes", *Journal of the American Institute of Planners,* Vol. 45, No. 1 (January, 1979), pp. 36-47.

Detwyler, Thomas P., and Marcus, Melvin G. (editors), *Urbanization and Environment: The Physical Geography of the City.* Belmont, Cal.: Duxbury Press, (1972) (Especially pp. 3-68).

Dickinson, Robert E., "The Growth of the Historic City," *The West European City: A Geographical Interpretation,* London, Poutledge and Kegan Paul, Ltd. (1951) pp. 270-300.

Greenberg, M. R., Anderson, R., and Page, G. W., *Environmental Impact Statements.* Resource Papers for College Geography, No. 78-3. Washington: Association of American Geographers, (1978), 35 pp.

Griggs, Gary B. and Gilchrist, John A., *The Earth and Land Use Planning.* North Scituate, Mass.: Duxbury Press. (1977) (Especially Chap. 2: Land Use Planning and Environmental Impact"), pp. 396-456.

Hewitt, Kenneth and Burton, Ian, *The Hazardousness of a Place: A Regional Ecology of Damaging Events.* Toronto, University of Toronto Press, (1971) (Especially p. 3-30).

Keller, Edward A., *Environmental Geology.* Columbus, Ohio: Charles E. Merrill Publishing Company, (1976).

Landsberg, Helmut E., *The Urban Climate.* New York: Academic Press, (1981).

Legget, Robert F., *Cities ad Geology,* New York, McGraw-Hill (1973).

Leveson, David, *Geology and the Urban Environment.* New York, Oxford University Press, (1980).

Marcus, Melvin G., et. al., *Urbanization and Environment,* Belmont, California, Duxbury Press (1972).

Marsh, William M., *Environmental Analysis for Land Use and Site Planning*. New York, McGraw-Hill Book Co., (1978) (Especially pp. 49-161).

Morgan, Donald, et. al., "Microclimates Within an Urban Area", *Annals of The Association of American Geographers*, Vol. 67, No. 1 (March, 1977), pp. 55-65.

Sutter, Ruth E., *The Next Place You Come To*, Englewood Cliffs, New Jersey, Prentice-Hall (1973).

U.S. Department of Housing and Urban Development, *Environmental Planning and Geology*, Washington, D.C. (1969).

Utgard, R. O., McKenzie, G. D., and Foley, D. (editors), *Geology in the Urban Environment*. Minneapolis, Burgess Publishing Co., (1978) (Especially pp. 3-8; 31-40; 85-101 and 302-323).

White, Gilbert F., et. al., *Changes in Urban Occupance of Flood Plains in the United States*. University of Chicago Department of Geography Research Paper No. 57, (1958) (Especially pp. 1-48 and 203-235).

White, Gilbert F., (editor), *Natural Hazards: Local, National, Global*. New York, Oxford University Press, (1974) (Especially pp. 1-16 and 187-205).

CHAPTER FIVE

Residential Land Use

Housing and Land

Land values in American cities generally decline outward from the city center. Reasons have been suggested why the poor live on the high-priced land and the rich on the lower-priced land. There are, however, anomolies in the land value curve, resulting from relative locations of things or from amenity values.

Commercial and industrial uses affect the value of nearby residential land, as do major thoroughfares, and large institutions, such as universities. People wish to live close to these other uses, but not too close. Residential land values are lower than normal for their relative location within about a quarter of a mile of many of these other uses and higher than normal for their relative location from about a quarter mile to about two miles. Residential land values may be higher, on the other hand, in proximity to certain other non-residential uses such as parks, country clubs, and institutional areas such as university campuses. All the anomolies suggested in previous chapters and in the preceeding paragraphs are generalities, however, for many other factors can affect residential land values at specific locations.

The type of structure on the land can raise or lower the land value, as also can nearby structures. The age and condition of the neighborhood and of

DISTANCE DECAY

RESIDENTIAL LAND VALUE PROFILE
ALONG A SUBURBAN CORRIDOR

Fig. 3

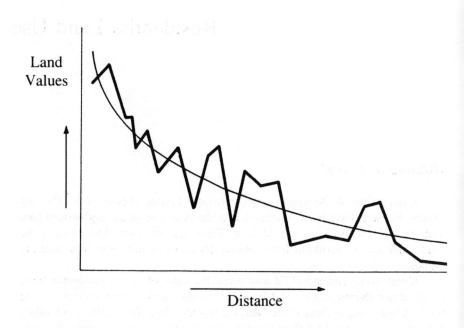

The basic shape of the distance decay curve is negative exponential (Fig. 1). However, there are so many anomolies along this seven mile stretch of commuter corridor that the line indicating the residential land value profile is quite jagged.

RESIDENTIAL LAND VALUE
CROSS SECTIONS

Fig. 4

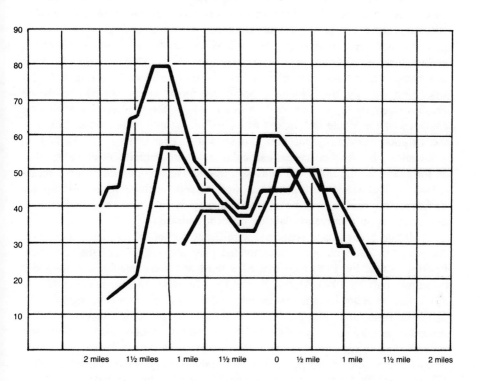

The diagram above represents three residential land value cross sections along a major suburban commuting corridor. The highest values are nearest the central city, the lowest the farthest away. This, again, illustrates the distance decay of land values outward from the city. (Fig. 1 and Fig. 3). The diagram also illustrates the land value anomolie associated with a high speed transport route. Land values are much higher than normal, for the location, from about ½ mile to about 2 miles from the transport line but lower within a quarter of a mile of the line. People wish to live close, but not too close to a high speed transport line.

nearby neighborhoods are also significant. The perceived status of the neighborhood and of nearby neighborhoods are other factors affecting land values, as are internal and external access, proximity to mass transit and major highways, availability of city services, distance from desirable functions, and the perceived status of the public schools which serve the neighborhood. It has even been said by some land economists that residential properties on the north and west sides of cities tend to be of high value while those on the south and east sides are more often than not of lower value. A parcel of land, with or without a structure, is worth whatever someone is willing to pay for it.

The architectural style of a house is visible evidence of culture. However, architecture is difficult to classify because of its great variety. In some instances, architectual style reflects the culture of a distinctive group of people who first occupy the structure. Some American urban neighborhoods are characterized by styles imported from abroad, as for example the distinctive rooflines of Lawndale in Chicago which reflect the origins in central Europe of the original residents, and the "Polish flats" characteristic of portions of Milwaukee. In other instances, particular styles are reminiscent of earlier eras, as for example, the many old houses in upstate New York which have Grecian columns. The exterior materials, as well as style, exhibit local and regional differences: some regions have predominantly brick, stone, or wood houses, depending upon relative availability of local materials.

Mobile homes have become a significant portion of the housing stock of America. In 1965 mobile homes totaled only about a fifth of the residential housing starts; by 1980 they totaled a third and some predict that they will constitute half by 1990. Mobile homes have become the poor man's castle. In 1965 the median income of mobile home dwellers was not significantly different from that of the U.S. total population in similar categories. (i.e. retired or employed)   By 1980 median incomes of mobile home residents had fallen to two thirds of that of the U.S. average in similar categories, and mobile homes accounted for 90 per cent of all single family homes valued at under $20,000 and 98 per cent of all single family homes valued at under $15,000.

Do mobile homes have to be so ugly? The answer is "no", but design costs money. The average mobile home only costs about two thirds that of a single family house but a series of designer mobile homes, put on the market a few years ago, cost within 10 per cent of the cost of a pre-cut house and they did not sell.

Must mobile homes be vulnerable to fire (inadequate wiring, flammable materials, inadequate escape, etc) and wind (top heavy, light, inadequate anchor)? The answer is no, but safety costs money. Nevertheless, many states have tightened construction codes and it is anticipated that the federal government will soon step in with an over-all code for mobile homes.

Many city planners are very negative about mobile homes. They point out that mobile homes pay less tax and depreciate very rapidly, becoming slums in a short time. Mobile home defenders counter that perhaps they should pay less tax inasmuch as they use less land than typical conventional houses and only produce, on the average, one school child for every three produced by single family housing. Further, say the mobile home spokesman, rapid depreciation is an asset inasmuch as housing can be renewed and slums eliminated with much greater frequency.

Most American cities have multi-unit residential buildings, generally predominating in the older neighborhoods, in inner-city localities which have been subjected to urban renewal, in sectors of high-income near shorelines and other special situations, and in recently-developed clusters in the outer portions of cities and in some suburbs.

In most instances, the styles of multiple-unit residential buildings tend to reflect the periods during which they were built, rather than local or regional differences.

Many cities have neighborhoods of two-unit buildings, sometimes called "duplexes", with the units either side-by-side or one over the other. Such neighborhoods tend to have higher population densities than those of neighborhoods where single-unit detached houses predominate. Much of the popularity of duplex housing, which has recently had a revival in some cities, is due to economic reasons: owner-occupancy of one of the units is within economic reach because the rental collected from the other unit goes a long way toward paying the mortgage obligation and the taxes on the owner-occupied unit. In many instances, the two units are occupied by two generations or branches of the same family.

During the early decades of the twentieth century, until the slowup of residential building in the 1930's, some of the largest American cities were characterized by distinctive types of multiple-unit residential structures, generally called "apartment" buildings. Local ordinances in most instances place the lower size limit at three or five units; building codes and, later, zoning ordinances, made residential structures of a given number of stories subject to additional costly restrictions, such as fire resistance and provision of elevators. Many old and middle-aged Chicago neighborhoods, for example, have predominantly three-story apartment buildings, while neighborhoods developed during the same periods in New York City are characterized by six-story apartment buildings, with or without elevators.

After World War II, the "garden apartment" became popular. This type of residential development consists of low-rise (usually two or three stories) buildings covering only a small portion of the site area, with open space devoted to landscaped areas, playgrounds and recreational space and offstreet parking occupying the remainder of the site. The garden apartment implies larger than conventional lots; this necessitated in many instances a new form of zoning regulation - the P.U.D. or "planned unit development." PUD regulations also facilitate residential areas with mixtures of structural types in planned spatial arrangements; single-unit detached houses, duplexes, single-unit attached houses (termed "row" houses, "group" houses, or ''town'' houses), low-rise (two and three story apartment buildings) and, in some instances, high-rise buildings as well. In some of the larger PUD's non-residential facilities, such as schools, convenience shopping areas, and church sites, may be provided; in many cases the provision of such sites by the developer is mandatory.

Generally speaking, the value of a residential structure reflects in part, the value of the land on which it is built, which, in turn, is closely related to access. However, many factors can affect housing value. One widely used measure is structural condition, often called housing quality.

Housing quality is related to the protectional qualities of a house. Protection against the elements is an important function of a house, though not necessarily the most important function.

For the purpose of classifying structural condition, a housing unit is a house, apartment or other group of rooms, or a single room that is occupied or intended to be occupied as separate living quarters. Condition is categorized as sound, deteriorating, dilapidated, or condemnable.

Rating of structural condition is an ongoing activity for most city governments. Inspectors armed with check lists go into the field and observe footings and foundations, walls, roofs, porches and steps, windows and doors, chimneys, plumbing, wiring, flashing, and fire hazards. Points are assigned and added together to categorize a house, from sound to condemnable. Houses are aggregated by neighborhood so the city government can keep constant watch on housing and neighborhood condition.

Physical deterioration is the most obvious and observable factor in housing obsolence. There are, however, other reasons for obsolence, even abandonment. Obsolete style or function can render a dwelling unit less desirable. Neighborhood decline can have a negative effect on housing desirability. Overcrowding within the housing unit is an important factor in deterioration. Even credit constraints or the property tax system can make maintenance difficult and thus contribute to dwelling unit obsolesence.

Other housing problems include inequitable distribution, segregation and discrimination, affordability, and needs for special groups (e.g. elderly, handicapped, transients, etc).

Neighborhoods

''Neighborhood'' is an inexact term. City planners often draw neighborhood boundaries to conform to census boundaries so that data for description, comparison, and analysis are readily available. Perceptual studies indicate that residents generally designate a smaller area than do planners, and they base delineation on perceived social and economic factors. Planners usually include shopping areas, schools, parks, churches, etc. in a neighborhood; residents do not necessarily include them.

HOUSING AFFORDABILITY

Percent of U.S. families who can afford to buy an averaged priced house.

Fig. 5

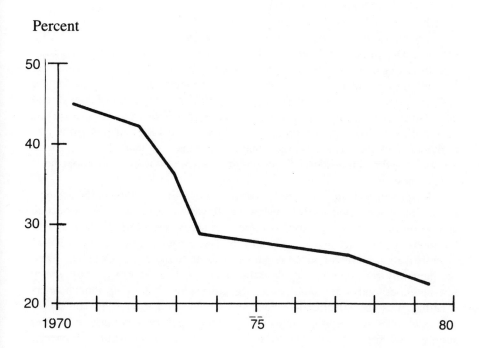

The graph above indicates the extremely high inflationary trend in housing cost and interest rates vs. the slower rise in expendable income. There is very recent evidence that housing cost is increasing at a decreasing rate but incomes must do considerable "catching up" before families, other than those with upper incomes, can afford to buy housing.

One scholar suggested three types of common awareness neighborhoods: acquaintence, homogenous, and unit. An acquaintence neighborhood is one in which people know each other or at least know who their neighbors are. An homogenous neighborhood is usually larger than an acquaintence neighborhood and is one where the houses are of similar size, price, condition, or they look alike. The unit neighborhood is the largest of the three and more like the planners' neighborhood. It contains shopping facilities, schools, parks, churches, and other land uses accessory to housing.

The concept of "neighborhood" was developed by the New York City Planning Department in 1909 as a planning tool. The New York neighborhood was envisioned as a cellular area dominated by an elementary school and separated from adjacent neighborhoods by shopping streets. Except for the addition of curved access streets, and cul de sacs and placement of commercial and institutional functions near the center of the neighborhood, the structure of neighborhoods has changed little. The cellular morphology of modern neighborhoods and the inward-facing situation remains a potent force for socioeconomic and racial residential segregation. "Birds of a feather flock together" then as now.

Neighborhoods do, of course, change through time. Although the ecological analogue suggested by Robert Park — "invasion-succession-climax-decline and so on in a circular fashion" — does not necessarily reflect reality, neighborhoods do decline, and occasionally revive, through what has been called "gentrification." Such revived neighborhoods are termed "cosmopolitan" and are generally regarded as very desirable places to live. However, only a very few neighborhoods are candidates for "gentrification." Housing, though deteriorating, must be structurally sound and the location must offer convenient access to amenities. Further, housing in the metropolitan area must be in short supply, and the city must be relatively free from racial strife. Of course, mortgage money must also be available to potential buyers. Unfortunately, these conditions do not guarantee gentrification, they only permit it. If a neighborhood "gentifies" and become "cosmo" the qualities that bind the residents together tend to be intellectual or artistic rather than economic.

The influx of Blacks has unjustly been accorded much of the blame for decline of many neighborhoods. Replacement of white residents by Blacks is usually by diffusion: blacks from one neighborhood expand into adjacent neighborhoods while during the same period the original predominantly Black neighborhood has attained an even higher proportion of Blacks.

The typical assumption of Black expansion is: threat-decline-recovery-decline. The actuality is decline-penetration-recovery. Studies have shown that predominantly Black neighborhoods, recently encroached, show higher rates of property appreciation, over the same period, than comparable all-white neighborhoods. Property owners simply believe that their properties are worth more than they really are in a neighborhood that has already started its decline. Thus in many cities, abetted by discrimination, there is a dual housing market,

BLACK RESIDENTIAL ENCROACHMENT

Fig. 6

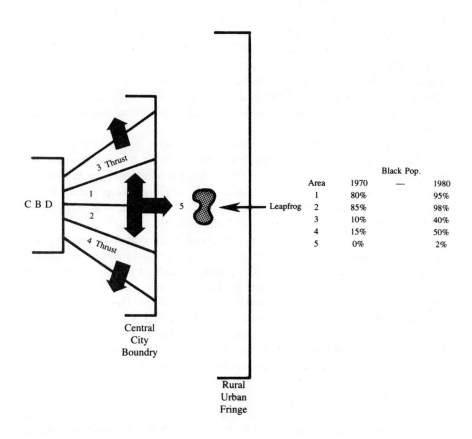

Area	Black Pop. 1970	—	1980
1	80%		95%
2	85%		98%
3	10%		40%
4	15%		50%
5	0%		2%

Black residential areas increase through expansion. Many predominantly black areas in 1970 have become almost entirely black by 1980. Partially black areas in 1970 have increased the ratio of blacks significantly by 1980. However, there is some leapfrogging.

with Blacks and other non-Whites paying much more than Whites for equivalent housing.

Numerous studies have shown that racial riots tend to occur midway between the old ghetto cores and the advancing ghetto margins. It is in such areas between the relatively prosperous advancing front and the declining older core that relative deprivation is most severe; that expectation for space is not fulfilled by the environment, that inadequate housing is seen as an attack against health, safety, and comfort, and that police practices are perceived as attacks against dignity. As Black neighborhoods expand, congestion tends to increase because population increases, in many instances, faster than the supply of land and housing. It is midway between the old ghetto core and the advancing ghetto margins that the relative deprivation of space is most severe. Ghetto is defined as "ethnic enclave" and is not synonimous with "slum." Black ghetto is the proper term to describe predominantly Black neighborhoods. Other racial, national, and religious groups may also be clustered, either voluntarily or involuntarily, and in that sense the areas which they occupy may be "ghettos." However, abut 90 percent of poverty in many cities is among Blacks.

Black ghettos formed, in the United States, after World War I with the first large scale Black migrations from the South to the northeastern and midwestern cities. Prior to that time, Blacks lived in small enclaves in cities, or side-by-side with Whites. The impetus for migration was furnished by expanded industrial employment opportunities. The push was agricultural mechanization resulting in a surplus of farm workers.

Blacks, as the most recent, poorest, and least skilled of the migrants generally had no alternative except to settle in cities, into slums that already existed. These slums were in the most centrally-located and oldest areas. As they expanded, Whites moved out. In fact researchers have noted that the "tipping point" is somewhere between ten and twenty-five per cent Black occupancy; that is, when the proportion of Blacks in a neighborhood exceeds these ratios, Whites move out in increasing numbers. Black leaders say that those conditions are a result of White decisions that have kept Black people inferior, and that these conditions can only be changed by another series of decisions by Whites.

Neighborhood decline is a constant threat to cities. As a neighborhood declines, former residents move outward and less affluent people enter. This succession of residents is termed "filtering down", and it has been the method by which less affluent people have been able to find housing. When you think about it, though, filtering down is a "do it yourself" slum-maker. As the decline process continues, neighborhood skill level and purchasing power decline, and commercial and institutional establishment close or relocate elsewhere. As an area deteriorates, tax revenues decline or become uncollectable, and the city loses both economic base and tax base.

There are certain characteristics that indicate potential neighborhood decline. Among them are:

1. Detrimental mixtures of incompatible land uses such as a bar next to a church next to a store next to a house.

2. Instability of population or function: A high ratio of families moving in and out and a large number of stores and offices changing function or proprietors.

3. Little demand for housing: houses that do not sell as well as in other neighborhoods or cannot even be rented immediately.

4. Poor internal or external accessibility: barriers to or circuitous access routes into and out of the neighborhood and difficult travel conditions within the neighborhood.

5. Inadequate revenues to support the required public services.

6. Lack of neighborhood pride, and hence insufficient political "clout", combined with inability to attract sufficient private capital: that is when a city councilman or an important industrialist wants to locate a potentially noxious industrial plant within the neighborhood and residents do not oppose it, future neighborhood decline is probable.

It is not always possible for a city to act in order to halt neighborhood decline, even though the characteristics noted above are well known. There are early signs of neighborhood decline that can be observed by residents or city officials. Among them are:

1. High ratio of renters to owners: if many residential units are tenant-occupied rather than owner-occupied, especially if increase in tenant-occupancy has occured recently.

2. Commercial establishments do not adapt to the neighborhood, and commercial proprietors no longer live in the neighborhood.

3. Absence of extensive renovation of deteriorating dwelling units: even if only two or three houses in the neighborhood are deteriorating and rehabilitation is not taking place, it is likely the neighborhood has started its decline.

4. Location of noxious functions within the neighborhood: if a polluting industrial plant has been built in the neighborhood, decline has likely started.

Neighborhood quality has an influence on quality of life, though not the only influence. It might be said that quality of life or social well-being is the goal of all human endeavor. If that is so, we must learn to measure quality of life before steps can be taken to improve it.

Measurement of "social well-being" or "quality of life" has been attempted many times. The concept of measuring spatial differentiation of life quality is important, even exciting. The actuality has been less than satisfactory.

The usual method has been to select a number of variables as surrogates for quality-of-life, and to collapse them into statistical indicators. The variables selected are usually measures of income, housing, education, employment, health, creature comforts and so on. Variables are limited to the measurable and the measured. Since most of these data are from the censuses, they lean heavily on economic factors and often ignore factors that might better indicate true social well-being.

Perhaps the *a priori* theorizing regarding life quality, employed by some scholars, better reflects social well-being than do measurable indicators. Perhaps the interview method employed by some scholars truly reflects social well-being. After all, if most respondents in a place agree that "life is good" could they be that far off?

Neighborhood Renewal

Private neighborhood renewal has worked well in a few small areas within cities. The "gentrification" of cosmopolitan and university neighborhoods has brought middle and upper-middle income people back into the city and has renewed these few neighborhoods. Life-cycle moves have brought, to a limited degree, middle-income people back into the city, sometimes into gentrified areas, but more often to close-in middle and upper-middle cost apartments and "town houses." These centripital forces, however, are extremely rare compared to the centrifigal, counter-urbanization, forces. Movement back to the city is a trickle compared to outward movement.

Private neighborhood renewal is difficult to accomplish. Most people don't want to be "pathbreakers" by investing in a dwelling unit within a neighborhood that has obviously declined. Also, banks and savings and loan establishments are reluctant to issue mortgages for houses in such areas unless the neighborhood shows positive signs of gentrification. In fact, though it is vigorously denied by most lenders, "red-lining" is commonly practiced. Red-lining simply means that red lines are drawn on a map enclosing areas within which mortgage money will not be made available.

The answer to neighborhood renewal in the United States has been public urban renewal. The several acts provide federal matching funds to upgrade eligible areas within cities. These areas need not be residential, although most of the renewed areas have been predominantly residential.

The renewal programs fell into three categories: clearance, spot clearance and partial rebuilding, and rehabilitation.

Clearance involves the purchase of land and buildings, complete clearance and resale or long-term lease to developers. The developers must redevelop the area in accordance with a pre-arranged plan.

Spot clearance and partial rebuilding involves the purchase and removal of only the buildings where individual structures are beyond repair. These buildings are demolished and the land sold or leased to a developer for spot renewal according to a plan.

Rehabilitation involves low-cost or no-cost (depending on family income) loans to home owners to enable them to improve structures up to sound condition.

In all three programs the city must rate the structures according to federal and state guidelines and make an official declaration as to the condition of the areas, again following federal and state guidelines.

Although the federal renewal program has had insufficient funding for several years, there are still many projects under way or under contract.

Opponents of urban renewal voice several objectives to the program and, in fact, to the concept:

1. The program is slow. The average time for a project from start to completion has been twelve years. As a result, housing deteriorates faster than renewal takes place.

2. The program does not help the original residents, who generally cannot afford to return to the area following its renewal.

3. The program reduces the total number of housing units, on the average by one-third in a typical renewal area.

4. The program eliminates many commercial and industrial establishments that can exist nowhere else or, at the very least, it drives them out of the city.

5. Police departments do not want slum dwellers, whom they consider to be crime-prone, dispersed throughout the city. Police would prefer them agglomerated in a few small areas.

Proponents of urban renewal counter with the following points:

1. The program was never primarily intended to provide low-cost housing, but rather to facilitate the filtering-down process, and it has generally been successful in this regard.

2. Slums are crime-breeders and are physically dangerous.

3. Slum areas do not produce taxes sufficient to pay for services which they require.

4. Perhaps most important say the proponents, we should quit punishing the poor with inferior housing, inferior education, inferior status, and the final indignity: telling them how they may and may not spend aid money.

Perhaps most puzzling to middle-class people (most social scientists, public officials, and planners are middle-class people) is the apparent fact that slum-dwellers do not seem to want to move to better housing. Some studies indicate that about two-thirds of these people would prefer not to move. Reasons involve low rent, spatial identity (it is home), kinship ties, environmental stability (i.e. little transient population), and most important, the social life and protection of the street. They perceive not only safety in numbers but also enjoyment. Yet, many scholars point to crowding as a debilitating aspect of slum living.

Crowding, some researchers believe, is a contributing factor to delinquincy, sexual deviation, violence, and ultimately death from shock due to constant over stimulation of the adrenal glands. These scholars point to studies of animals where crowding leads to these very effects.

Crowding, other researchers maintain, is not necessarily associated with pathological conditions, nor with stress, provided it is not accompanied by certain other conditions. Furthermore, crowding actually helps to control crime and deviant behavior through the "eyes on the street" syndrome. These researchers point to the high-income high-density multi-family neighborhoods in the United States, Japan, and Western Europe that have very low crime rates. In fact, they say, cities of Western Europe and Japan were re-built after the devastation of World War II to accomodate the same high densities as pre-war housing. Partly this was necessary because of scarce land but do the Western Europeans and Japanese know something about pleasant living that Americans have not yet discovered? It is more satisfactory to live close to other people?

United States federal guidelines put dwelling unit crowding at anything more than one person per room. For example, if a dwelling unit has kitchen, living room, dining room, two bedrooms and bath (not counted as a room) it can accomodate five permanent residents. This seems reasonable, although it must also be said that evidence associating crowding with deviant behavior is inconclusive.

Public urban renewal is an official attempt to replace or rehabilitate neighborhoods. Its proponents say it has been successful in the endeavor, although too slowly. Its critics say it has done more harm than good, and they suggest alternatives.

One suggested partial alternative to urban renewal is urban homesteading. Based on the homesteading of frontier days, the city buys deteriorating housing in declined neighborhoods, with federal aid, and resells the structure and land to a homesteader for a small payment. The homesteader must live in the house for four years before he acquires title. During the period he must bring the structure up to standard through low cost government loans and much "elbow grease." The program is successful and exciting for those few people involved, but is miniscule compared to the millions of dwelling units in the United States which are in need of rehabilitation.

Another suggested alternative to urban renewal is public ownership of all land and buildings within a city. Proponents of this alternative point out that one or another government owns about half the land at any given time and thus needs only to purchase the other half. They suggest that government ownership of land in the British new towns and in Sweden has worked well. If the city owned the land and buildings and leased them on various terms, say the proponents, there would be a constant, ongoing partnership between leaser and leasee. The financial problems associated with this proposed program are, however, enormous and politically impossible. The United States economy is built on the foundation of private capital, as is the country's tax structure.

Yet another suggested alternative to urban renewal is increased building inspection, in which city building inspectors would inspect all buildings at least every other year. Home owners and landlords would be warned, as a dwelling unit deteriorated. If rehabilitation did not take place, the building would finally be condemned, and tenants evicted. The hypothesis is that homeowners and landlords would be forced to maintain dwelling units to standard. It would seem that proponents of this scheme fail to anticipate the hordes of displaced persons marching on city hall or the corpses lying about after a particular cold night. Many people cannot afford to rehabilitate a structure.

Although the U.S. federal Urban Renewal Program would seem to be on its way out, other programs are offered. For example, there is the Urban Development Action Grant (UDAG) program. UDAG makes low cost government loans available to developers in certain specified urban areas. Projects presumably must serve the dual purpose of urban renewal and job creation.

Public Housing

The purpose of urban renewal is neighborhood rehabilitation. One of the purposes of public housing is the same. However, public housing units are publicly owned, newly built structures rented to low-income families. There are several programs for construction but they all result in rent-subsidized housing for low income families.

It is generally not feasible for a low income family to build or purchase a house. The Federal Housing Administration insists a family cannot afford a house more costly than two and one half times gross annual family income. Obviously, there are few homes available for purchase by low income people. Even rents must reflect the value of a structure. In answer to this dilemma, public housing was initiated in order that housing-deprived families might have a decent place to live and that neighborhood rehabilitation might take place.

Criticism of the public housing program has been severe and continuous. Some of the criticism has resulted in program changes, some is surely in error, but some is valid and has yet to result in program change. A few of these criticisms follow:

Critics say that high-rise public housing units have become jungles, with terror in the vestibules, rape in the elevators, and murder in the playgrounds. Public housing defenders admit the high-rises have removed tenants from the "protection of the street" and suggest it is unlikely that many new high-rises will be built. By the late 1970s construction of high-rise public housing had virtually stopped.

Critics say that tenants have no pride of ownership and thus do not adequately care for the units. Public housing projects, therefore, tend to become slums quickly. Defenders say the reasons for this are two fold, both correctable. Tenants from the slums, say the defenders, have not been trained in the use of simple appliances (i.e. gas stoves, disposals, etc.) nor have they been schooled to expect rudimentary city services (i.e. solid waste collection,

police protection, etc.). These problems are easily eliminated through education. Pride of ownership can be engendered by permitting tenants to purchase
units under certain circumstances, say the defenders, and point out that this is
now possible for desirable tenants in certain places.

Critics say that to force public housing tenants to move when family
income rises above a certain level is counter-productive in that potential
community leaders are removed. Defenders agree and point out that it is now
possible, in certain projects, for higher income families to pay more rent and
remain or even to purchase the unit.

Another criticism is that massive projects perpetrate segregation and create
stigma. Defenders agree, and point out that the official policy of the
Department of Housing and Urban Development has changed from massive
projects to scattered-site public housing. Dispersing rent-subsidized housing
throughout the residential areas of a city is considered to be sound. Public furor
has arisen, however, on numerous occasions. Dissatisfaction has usually been
due to overloaded facilities (parks, schools, streets, public transit, e. al.).
Racial prejudice has also tended to inhibit scattered-site public housing.

One of the most serious and valid criticisms of public housing is that it has
tended to create a culture of perpetual tenants. People forced into rental housing
in the 1950's and 60's have a drawer full of rent receipts. On the other hand,
people who purchased housing, during the same period, needed a very low
down payment and acquired mortgages for between 5 and 10 per cent interest.
Housing has appreciated by nearly that much per year over the past two
decades. Further, interest payments and taxes are tax deductible. In effect, the
white middle-class homeowners lived rent-free while public housing tenants
paid rent. Further, it is not uncommon for a homeowner to walk away from a
sale with a hundred thousand dollars in his pocket that had grown from an
original $2,000 (down payment) investment of 20 years ago.* Thus, public
housing tenants were also denied the opportunity to accumulate capital.

Several alternatives to public housing have been suggested. Two of these
follow:

Direct rent subsidy has been suggested as a viable substitute for public
housing and indeed the program has been tested in pilot projects. The low-income family is sent a check each month, ostensibly for rental payment, but
actually to be used for any purpose. Critics of the program point out that, at
least in the pilot projects, most recipients did not move to better housing and
those who did tended to move to another sub-standard house. Defenders of the
program counter that the program should not be considered alternative to urban

---

*Land appreciates, structures depreciate. A thirty year old house may be worth about half
its replacement cost. However, when the value of landscaping, outbuildings, and other
improvements is added to the appreciated value of the land, the result is one of overall
appreciation.

renewal or public housing but an adjunct to other social services and one that could operate without the costly infrastructure associated with other welfare payments. If the money is spent on family living, other funds are freed for rent. Perhaps the subsidy was too small to permit better housing.

A negative income tax has frequently been suggested as an alternative to not only public housing but to all welfare and even social security payments. The concept is simple; all shall have "X" number of dollars per year. If a person or family earns less, the Internal Revenue Service sends a series of monthly checks to bring income to X. Otherwise a tax is paid, as is now the case. Proponents note that the IRS is very efficient and could administer such a program much more inexpensively than the many public service agencies now operating.

According to its critics, a negative income tax would destroy initiative. The defenders maintain that the present welfare system destroys initiative. People with little skill cannot hope to hold a job long. They often perceive it to be better to never accept a job than to ultimately lose both welfare payments and a job.

Many of its critics say that the program would be too costly. The proponents indicate that each family of four could be brought up to an amount equal to the prorated cost of all social programs now operating.

A counter argument is that the program would keep people out of the labor market. They shouldn't be there, say the proponents. The bottom three or four per cent of the population cannot or will not work. Bidding them into jobs raises all wages and fuels inflation. Further, productivity is lowered by their presence. Those who don't work should starve, say some. The problem is, say the proponents, they refuse to starve happily. Some will surely prefer to acquire a "Saturday night special" and shoot you for the money in your pocket.

Finally, the critics of the negative income tax ask what will happen to all the welfare administrators thrown out of work by the program. This question remains unanswered by the proponents of the program.

In spite of all the problems of the so-called "inner-city" ghettos, by all available statistical indicators, whether it be crowding, sanitary facilities, or degree of deterioration of structures, the physical quality of housing is better than it was a generation or two ago. We must be careful to differentiate those negative conditions which are associated with the physical characteristics of residential areas and housing from those which are inherent in a society. Social and economic problems result from the presence of people. Improving the conditions of housing will reduce only a small part of the basic causes of social pathology; the ultimate solutions rest in the total society, not solely in housing.

Although there has been, in some instances and in highly localized areas, some up-grading of inner-city neighborhoods, the outward movement of population to and beyond the urban periphery persists in most American cities and metropolitan areas. The negative exponential "distance decay" curve of residential and land costs ("site rentals" and the "bid-rent curve" to use the terminology of the land economists) is as valid now as earlier, and socio-economic residential segregation, on the whole, persists. While the lower-status inner city areas may be occupied by Blacks, Hispanic-Americans, and more recently Asians and other minorities in contrast to the immigrants from Europe in earlier generations, the spatial patterns of blight, substandard housing, crime and other socio-economic pathology are not very different now than they were two or three generations ago. The same processes of peripheral expansion, neighborhood transition, ethnic and racial segregation whether voluntary or involuntary, are as valid and operational now as ever. Some of the forces and processes are inexorable; others can be modified to some degree by public policies and intervention, for better or for worse.

Intermediate Housing Stock

We now turn our attention to the extensive areas of most American cities in which nearly half of the population lives: the middle-aged and middle-quality residential areas which typically are situated between the old inner-city areas where physical and socio-economic deterioration is common, and the newer middle and upper-middle class city and suburban areas closer to the urban periphery. These are, for the most part, sprawling areas which are neither new or old; most of the housing was built between the beginning of the twentieth century and World War II. While some of the neighborhoods in these areas are characterized by populations with mixed racial, ethnic or socio-economic characteristics, many of them contain more homogenous populations of similar racial ethnic religions, nativity, educational and other qualities. Given a reasonable degree of choice, some people and families prefer to live in neighborhoods with a variety of neighbors, but more prefer to have neighbors much like themselves.

Many such areas, immediate in location and in many characteristics between "inner city" and "suburbia" are of good physical quality: housing is generally adequate and properly maintained, and local facilities and services such as schools, churches, parks, playgrounds and local commercial establishments are present and reasonably adequate. On the other hand, the outward pressures from the central parts of the city, as inmigration of minorities continues and urban renewal uproots some people, as continued deterioration of inner city housing forces more people to move, and as civic projects result in additional residential clearance, pressures on middle-quality middle-aged residential areas make it imperative that the otherwise inevitable "filtering-down" of residential and neighborhood quality be resisted. Sooner or later, some structures will be less than adequately maintained; as they get older, maintenance becomes more difficult and more costly. Commercial establishments, in turn, will suffer from the consequent out-migration of residents who can afford better housing and residential environments and their replacement by lower-income people in the "filtered down" housing; the two types of population change are mutually reinforcing in producing lower incomes and hence lower commercial potential.

This downward spiral is not everywhere inevitable. In some communities and some cities there have been strong and successful programs of conservation and rehabilitation, which has slowed up, and even reversed, the downward trend. In some such areas partial and selective redevelopment of the most deteriorated clusters of buildings with replacement by new residential, commercial and/or institutional structures has stimulated additional public and private investment in the area as well as a renewed civic pride and a consequent generally higher level of maintenance of the existing housing inventory. Local leadership and political "clout" generally available to a greater extent than in most "inner city" areas, has often resulted in better levels of public services. "Grass roots" civic organizations in some instances have been effective in stimulating rehabilitation and conservation programs, and they may be effective instruments of two-way communication between relevent public agencies and business organizations on the one hand and the local residents on the other hand.

Because it is physically, economically, and politically impossible to replace more than a small portion of the housing stock and other facilities in most urban communities in a few years or even decades, it is especially important to maintain at a high level and to improve as much as possible those housing units and other structures which are too good to abandon or replace but which, if left alone, would eventually deteriorate, thus accelerating the encroachment of blight. Urban Americans, for the most part, must live in and with such housing for a long time to come.

On the other hand, more than three out of five of the housing units in the United States in the early 1980s were built since the end of World War II. The single-family detached house on a quarter-acre lot was the preponderant status symbol and aspiration of a high proportion of American families during most of the period, until, in the 1970's, the rapidly-increasing cost of motor fuel together with the inflation and its high cost of mortgage money made it evident that fewer families could realize that ambition.

The past few decades have seen the rise of large-scale residential developers and mass-producing housing. Because of physical, economic and institutional constraints, most single-family detached housing was constructed in the outer areas of cities, in the burgeoning suburbs, or in open country which rapidly became suburbanized. Except for a limited number of publicly-assisted high-density urban renewal projects, most large-scale developments were on formerly open land, or on low-density non-residential land converted to residential use from institutional uses, general aviation airports, and golf courses, and, of course farmland. Government assistance, in the form of mortgages guaranteed by the Federal Housing Administration or the Veterans Administration against losses by the financial institutions in the event of default, permitted long-term lower-interest financing to be available to millions of families who otherwise could not afford such housing. The full impact of the federal housing programs initiated during the 1930's was delayed by the Great Depression and by World War II. After the War, however, the pent-up demand due to the low rate of housing construction for nearly two decades combined with the postwar baby boom to produce, literally, an explosion of cities and metropolitan areas into the countryside. The metropolitan explosion was exacerbated by other federal and in some instances State policies which, combined with rising affluence, stimulated migration from the older inner areas of cities to the outer areas and beyond, into suburbia and exurbia. Among the catalysts for the outward movement were programs of land clearance and urban renewal and the clearance of extensive city areas for expressways implementing the federal housing acts of 1949 and 1954 and the Interstate Highway Act of 1956, among other programs. Few low-income people or families, especially Blacks and other minorities who lived in the "inner city" deteriorated areas, could afford to move to the new suburbs or, in most instances, to the increasingly scarce - and hence costly - housing that remained in the inner areas of the cities, or even of many of the older suburbs. The high-rise high-density public housing projects in many cities proved, in retrospect, to be as undesirable, for the most part, as the overcrowded, deteriorated housing which they partially replaced. They tend to concentrate social problems and promote racial segregation to an even greater extent than previously. One of the largest such public housing developments, Pruitt-Igoe in St. Louis, hailed originally as an ideal prototype, proved to be such a disaster that it was actually blasted out of existence a decade after it was built.

Somewhat better than out-and-out public housing, which was greatly expanded under Title III of the Housing Act of 1949, was publicly-aided urban redevelopment housing under Title I of that act to redevelop portions of the deteriorated inner city areas for housing to be occupied by middle-income families, mainly those who chose not to live in suburban locations. But Title I housing, such as Lake Meadows, Praire Shores, and Carl Sandburg Village in Chicago, Juneau Village in Milwaukee, and many others, were not sufficiently low-rental for the former residents of the sites, nor were the resulting densities as high as those formerly in the same areas. The catalytic effects in stimulating additional renewal activity adjacent to or near the sites of such projects were, in general, less than anticipated.

The result of these "pushes" from central city areas combined with outward "pulls" to produce a substantial lowering of residential densities in most American cities and metropolitan areas. Lower-income people, uprooted from centrally-located neighborhoods tended, in large part, to relocate in the extensive "filtered down" housing in the surrounding middle-aged areas. In some cities, such as Chicago, such areas had been occupied by half of the population and extended over half of the total expanse of land within the municipal limits. Pressures on these areas, increased by the housing demands of people uprooted from residences closer to the centers of the cities, tended to produce overcrowding, inadequate conversions, and neglect and consequent deterioration, of the housing stock and neighborhoods which, prior to such pressures, were still relatively good. In many instances the in-migrants were of minority groups, and racial tensions during the transition period produced explosive conditions. The racial disturbances of the mid-to-late 1960's were largely in such transition areas. In a few instances a more orderly change, with at least temporary "integration" was facilitated by enlightened neighborhood organizations formed for the purpose; they had a greater chance of success where an established large institution, such as a university or a cluster of hospitals in a "medical center" constituted a nucleus.

The public programs to provide low and middle income housing in the inner cities on the one hand, and in outer areas and suburbs on the other hand, thus had both positive and negative effects. Much of the worst housing in many parts of cities was eliminated, but commonly at the cost of disrupting or eliminating viable socially-cohesive neighborhoods and communities. Overcrowding is much less of a social problem now than it was three or four decades ago, except in some of the ill-conceived massive low-rent public housing clusters. The worst deteriorated residential structures are largely gone. The housing stock, on the whole, is much newer and of better quality than before. Conservation and rehabilitation measures, in many instances, have arrested the threatened decline of some intermediate, middle-aged areas, although others are still threatened with decline as rising affluence on the part of present occupants and migration outward to newer and better housing combines with "filtering down" of the housing units to accommodate the newer immigrants both to the cities and outward from the inner urban areas.

Suburbia, on the other hand, is the "catchment" area for the majority of movers and, until very recently, for the majority of newly-formed families. FHA and VA guaranteed loans brought single-unit houses within reach of almost everyone except the very poor. On the other hand, these programs in many instances tended to accelerate the decline of the intermediate as well as the poorer areas of the central cities and older suburbs, because the guaranteeing agencies as well as the financial institutions, banks, savings and loan organizations and insurance companies, undertook to issue mortgages only in areas of minimal risk, thus "red-lining" — refusing to finance — development or improvement where the risk was greater; such were the older areas, commonly when the residents were of minority racial or ethnic groups who could least afford good housing.

Many social commentators and observers pointed out, and generally lamented, the stereotyped homogeneous suburban communities of postwar America. However, in spite of their shortcomings, such suburbs offered many economic, social, political, and psychological advantages to their residents. They epitomized the general rising affluence, but at a cost. The decreases of central-city population created loss of income for city governments and for downtown commercial and service establishments. City-suburban frictions tended to inhibit the optimal organizational forms for providing many essential services. Civic leaders, in many instances being suburbanites, were not available to serve on the municipal boards and commissions of the central cities. And, of course, until suburban centers of employment caught up with deconcentration of population, ever-longer trips between home and work increased the demand for highways, cars, and extensions of utilities.

Not all suburbs are entirely, or even predominantly, residential. Many incorporated municipalities are basically commercial or industrial. Numerous establishments including industries, shopping centers, and public and private institutions, furnish employment and are workplace destinations for the residents of the community as well as those living in other parts of the urban region. Many establishments are located in unincorporated suburban and exurban areas, and similarly constitute nucleii of traffic generation for city, suburban and exurban residents. In some metropolitan areas, "reverse" commuting from central cities to peripheral employment locations is increasing rapidly. In such instances, the outlying employment adds to another impetus to the trend for residential movement to and beyond the urban periphery.

The urban form which is emerging in many instances as a result of these trends is a multinucleated urban area, with considerable reverse commuting from central-city residential locations as well as cross-commuting from outlying residential locations to outlying employment sites. The "urban sprawl" which many urbanists lamented is beginning to take a new form.

SELECTED READINGS

Barber, Gerald M., "Urban Population Distribution Planning", *Annals of the Association of American Geographers*, Vol. 68, No. 2 (June 1977) pp. 239-245.

Bourne, Larry S., *The Geography of Housing*, New York, V.H. Winston and Sons (1981).

Brown, Marilyn A., "Do Central Cities and Suburbs Have Similar Dimensions of Need?" *The Professional Geographer*, Vol. 32, No. 4 (Nov. 1980) pp. 410-411.

Bruba, William C., "Living the Good Life Near Transit Stations," *Planning*, Vol. 46, No. 4, (April 1980) pp. 20-21.

Cassidy, Robert, "The Needed Revolution in Mobile Homes," *Planning*, Vol. 39, No. 11, (Dec. 1973) pp. 12-18.

Clark, W.A.V., "Residential Mobility and Neighborhood Change et. al.," *Urban Geography*, Vol. I, No. 1 (Jan.-Mar. 1980)

Cox, Kevin R. and McCarthy, Jeffrey J., "Neighborhood Activism in the American City et. al.," *Urban Geography*, Vol. I, No. 1 (Jan.-Mar. 1980)

Cybriwsky, Rowan A., "Social Aspects of Neighborhood Change", *Annals of the Association of American Geographers*, Vol. 68, No. 1 (March 1968) pp. 17-35.

Dingemans, Dennis, "Redlining and Mortgage Lending in Sacramento," *Annals of the Association of American Geographers*, Vol. 69, No. 29 (June 1979) pp. 225-239.

Freedman, Jonathan L., *Crowding and Behavior*, San Francisco, W.H. Freeman & Co. (1975).

Gillard, Quentin, "The Effect of Environmental Amenities on House Values: The Example of a View Lot," *Professional Geographer*, Vol. 33, No. 2 (May 1981) pp. 216-220.

Grisby, William G. and Rosenburg, Louis, *Urban Housing Policy*, New York: APS Publications Inc., (1975).

Hall, Edward T., *The Hidden Dimension*, Garden City, N.Y., Doubleday & Co. (1966).

Hart, Graeme H.T., "Urban Residential Renovation and Renewal, et. al." *The Professional Geographer*, Vol. 32, No. 4 (Nov. 1980) pp. 439-445.

Harvey, David, *Society, The City and the Space-Economy of Urbanism,* Washington, D.C., Association of American Geographers, Resource Paper No. 18 (1972).

Hayes, Charles R., "Suburban Residential Land Values Along the C.B. & Q. Railroad," *Land Economics,* Vol. XXXIII, No. 2 (May 1957) pp. 177-181.

Hoyt, Homer, *The Structure and Growth of Residential Neighborhoods in American Cities,* Washington, D.C.: Federal Housing Administration, 1939.

Hoyt, Homer, *Where the Rich and the Poor People Live,* Washington, D.C., Urban Land Institute Technical Bulletin No. 55 (1966).

Johnston, R.J., *Urban Residential Patterns,* New York: Praeger Publishers, 1971.

Kain, John F. and Quigley, John M., "Measuring the Value of Housing Quality," *Journal of the American Statistical Association,* Vol. 65, (1970) pp. 537.

Koutsopoulos, K.C., "The Impact of Mass Transit on Residential Property Values", *Annals of the Association of American Geographers,* Vol. 67, No. 4 (Dec. 1977) pp. 564-576.

Lee, Terence, "Urban Neighborhood as a Socio-Spatial Schema," *Human Relations,* Vol. 21, No. 3 (1968) pp. 241-267.

Mayer, Harold M. and Wade, Richard C., *Chicago, Growth of a Metropolis,* Chicago, The University of Chicago Press (1969).

Mayer, Martin, *The Builders: Houses, People, Neighborhoods, Governments, Money,* New York: W.W. Norton & Co. Inc., (1978).

Morrill, Richard and Wohlenberg, Ernest, H., *The Geography of Poverty,* New York, McGraw Hill (1971).

Morrill, Richard L., "Stages in Patterns of Population Concentration and Dispersion," *The Professional Geographer,* Vol. 31, No. 1, (Feb. 1979) pp. 55-56.

Muller, Peter O., *The Outer City: The Geographical Consequences of the Urbanization of the Suburbs*. Association of American Geographers Resource Paper No. 75-2, Washington, (1976).

Muller, Peter O., *Contemporary Suburban America*, Englewood Cliffs, N.J. Prentice-Hall, Inc. (1981).

Muth, Richard, *Cities and Housing*, Chicago, University of Chicago Press (1969).

Patterson, John G., "Racial Inequality in Federal Housing Programs," *Southeastern Geographer*, Vol. 19, No. 2 (Nov. 1979) pp. 114-126.

Preston, Valerie and Taylor S. Martin, "Personal Construct Theory and Residential Choice," *Annals of the Association of American Geographers*. Vol. 71, No. 3 (Sept. 1981) pp. 437-451.

Pynoos, Job et. al., *Housing Urban America*, Chicago: Alolinc Publishing Co., (1973).

Rees, Philip, *Residential Patterns in American Cities*, Chicago, University of Chicago, Department of Geography Research Paper 189. (1979).

Rose, Harold M., *The Black Ghetto*, New York, McGraw Hill (1971).

Rubin, Barbara, "A Chronology of Architecture in Los Angeles," *Annals of the Association Geographers*, Vol. 67, No. 4, (Dec. 1977) pp. 521-537.

Smith, David M., *The Geography of Social Well-Being*, New York, McGraw Hill (1973).

Smith, Fred et. al. *Man and His Urban Environment*, New York, Man and His Urban Environment Project, Rockefeller Plaza (undated).

Thrall, Grant Ian, "A Geographic Criterion for Identifying Property-Tax Assessment Inequity," *The Professional Geographer*, Vol. 31, No. 3 (August 1979). pp. 278-283.

Wheaton, William L.C., et. al., (editors), *Urban Housing*, New York: The Free Press, (1966).

Wolf, Peter, *Land in America: Its Value, Use and Control*, New York: Pantheon Books, (1981).

Wolpert, Julian, et. al. *Metropolitan Neighborhoods: Participation and Conflict Over Change*, Washington, Association of American Geographer Resource Paper No. 16 (1972).

CHAPTER SIX

Commercial Land Use

"Commercial Land Use" includes a wide variety of establishments providing goods and services. The category includes retail establishments, offices of commercial and industrial firms, wholesale establishments where the stocking and warehousing of goods is less important than wholesale sales, and certain other types of establishments such as proprietary ("for profit") schools, hotels, motels, and commercial establishments furnishing entertainment and amusement. Some geographers and economists classify establishments as *primary* (those involved in extraction of both non-renewable and renewable resources), *secondary* (those involved in physical handling and distribution of goods, including processing, manufacturing, storing, and transportation), *tertiary* (those involved primarily in the transfer of ownership, including mainly wholesale and retail trade), and *quaternary* (those concerned with communication and record keeping). The great majority of commercial establishments are, under these definitions, tertiary and quaternary. In addition, many public functions have local characteristics and locations resembling commercial ones, although they are, perhaps erroneously, not considered as commercial land users.

In general, commercial land uses are far more important in the spatial patterns of cities and metropolitan areas than the relatively small extent of the lands they occupy would indicate.

Although the proportion of commercial land area to total urban area is generally small, it varies widely from city to city. In nearly every American city and almost every metropolitan area, commercial land use occupies less than five percent of the total land area, three percent is typical.

On the other hand commercial activities constitute major nodes in the urban pattern. They are essential foci, without which cities could not function. Both central and outlying commercial areas generate more daily trips by automobile and mass transit than do any other types of land uses, for both employment and shopping. The daily journey between home and work, more often than not, is to and from commercial areas in many cities, while retail establishments also generate heavy truck traffic.

In most American cities the core is still the commercial concentration downtown: The Central Business District, or CBD, although, increasingly in recent decades, outlying concentrations of offices and retail establishments are presenting effective competition.

Retailing

Walter Christaller's book, *The Central Places in South Germany*, entered the stream of geographic theory, very quietly, in 1933. It was designed to explain the size, nature, spacing, and location of towns in the belief that ordering principles governed those factors. These principles were subsequently found to be as applicable to the internal spatial patterns of cities and towns as they are to the inter-urban patterns. This "Central Place Theory" was destined to take its place with other theories of location.

The Central Place Theory is both more limited and more general than its author intended. Rather than being a theory of location of cities, it is a theory of retail and service activities. The theory has also been widely applied to the location of parks, new towns, public schools, and other urban functions although many applications beyond retailing and service do not fit the parameters of the theory. Nevertheless, the fact that planners and developers have successfully applied the theory to the real world, effectively argues its validity.

The theory provides much of the base for the geography of retailing and service, but there has been a tendency for geographers to be over impressed. The theory provides a stochastic analog or probability model of the mechanism of retailing. It does not tell us what a city is or how it operates internally beyond the retail and portions of the service sector. The theory assumes human behavior but cannot account for that human behavior which is not motivated by cost minimization. Throughfare service districts (retail strips along major routes catering to the motorist) do not conform to the theory nor do specialized retail areas (e.g., automobile rows, medical centers, skid row retailing, etc.). "Metropolitan Dominance" and "Dispersed Cities" also limit the central place theory in its application to the sizes and spacings of towns and cities.

Metropolitan Dominance offers a modification to the theory in regard to the spacing of urban centers. The Metropolitan Dominance concept points out that space between centers of the same rank increases with distance from a metropolis. This implies an increase of trade area size. The term "trade area" is used to describe a space, on the ground, surrounding a market, from which customers travel to obtain the goods and services of the market. The Metropolitan Dominance concept also points out the asymmetry of trade areas for centers close to a metropolis because these trade areas are pushed away from the larger center.

The Dispersed City Hypothesis identifies a group of closely spaced cities, of about the same size, with distances between them short enough for customers to choose any of several for shopping. Each of these cities merchandises convenience items locally but specializes in certain higher level goods and services. The urban nodes of a dispersed city, if considered an entity, would constitute a single economic unit and would presumably operate under the laws of the Central Place Theory but, as separate units, they do not.

The features of the Central Place Theory are as follows:

1. The basic function of a city is to provide goods and services to a surrounding trade area.*   In order to perform this function a city must be at the center of minimum aggregate travel, thus a "central place". Note that this statement exceeds reality. Centers that perform functions other than retailing (e.g., manufacturing, government, tourism, etc.) are larger than similar centers that perform only the retailing and service function.

2. Higher order places offer more goods, have more establishments and business types, serve larger trade areas and larger trade area populations, do greater volumes of business, and are more widely spaced, than lower order places.

3. Low order places provide only low order goods to a low order or small trade area. These low order goods are generally necessities (convenience goods) requiring frequent purchase with little consumer travel.

4. High order places provide not only low order goods and services, but also high order goods and services. Those high order goods are generally "shoppers' goods" for which the consumer is willing to travel longer distances, although less frequently. The higher the order of goods and services provided, the fewer are the establishments providing them, and the fewer and more widely spaced are the towns in which the establishments are located. Because higher order places offer more shopping opportunities and varieties, their trade areas are larger than those of low order places. Since consumers

---

*Other terms which are nearly synonymous with "trade area" are: hinterland, rimland, service area, umland, contributory area, complementary region, and the British terms, "urban field" and "catchment area."

have the opportunity to combine purposes on a single trip, this acts like a price reduction.

5. More specifically, central places fall into a hierarchy comprising discrete groups of centers. Centers of each higher order group perform all the functions of lower order centers plus a group of functions that differentiate them from and set them above, the lower order. A consequence of this is a nesting pattern of lower order trade areas within the trade areas of higher order centers, plus a hierarchy of routes joining the centers.

The term "trade area" has already been defined as a space, on the ground, surrounding a market, from which customers travel to obtain the goods and services of the market. However, it should be pointed out that since the "range" or market extent of each good and service varies, trade areas are an average or total accumulation of distance. If total accumulation or furthest extent is used as a trade area measure it is often called "reach." As markets rise in hierarchical level or increase in size, trade areas show a consequent increase in size. This occurs as new "thresholds" are reached. Threshold is the point at which a trade area can support a given function, or more simply, the purchasing power within a trade area necessary to the support of the supply of a particular good or service.

The Central Place Theory is obviously concerned with markets or the clustering of retail establishments in centers that are visited by customers. Customers presumably wish to conduct business with a minimum of cost and effort. Thus, they will travel only short distances to obtain items frequently used but less frequent purchases can be postponed so a single longer trip will accomplish several purposes. Therefore, a variety of central places will exist in any area. These different levels of central places might be called, from lowest to highest order: (1) hamlet, (2) village, (3) town, (4) small city, (5) regional city, (6) regional metropolis and (7) national metropolis. Since city size, as measured by population, is fairly closely associated with hierarchical level, population approximations have been attached to the different levels as follows: (1) 100, (2) 500, (3) 1,500, (4) 6,000, (5) 60,000, (6) 250,000, (7) 750,000 and over. Obviously, the lower the order of the center, the more numerous its occurance in space, therefore the shorter distance or time a customer need travel to reach it. There are normally more hamlets than villages, more villages than towns, more towns than cities, and so on. The question is: How many more and how are they arranged in space?

Christaller argued empirically for hexagonally shaped trade areas. Circles would either overlap or leave space between trade area boundaries. Squares would require considerably more travel from corners to center than from sides to center, although in areas such as the United States Midwest, where the road pattern is rectangular, trade areas may be rectangular. Christaller hypothesized that since the highest order center provides all goods, the next lower order center will locate at the mid-point between three of the high order centers. Repeating the argument leads to a hierarchy of centers. Every high order center

HEXAGONAL NETWORK

K = 3

Fig. 7

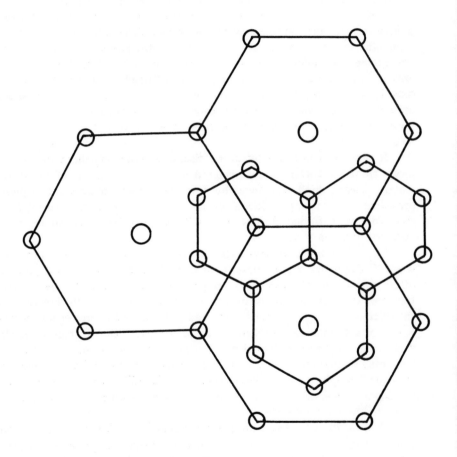

The diagram above represents the K=3 hexagonal lattice or network. Each center of the highest order is surrounded by a ring of six centers of the next lower order located at the six points of its hexagon. For every center there are three market areas of the next lower size for a progression of 1, 3, 9, 27, 81, 243, and 729. There are seven levels of market sizes.

is surrounded by a ring of six centers of next lower order located at the six points of its hexagon. For every center of the highest order, there are three market areas of next lower size. The progression of numbers of market areas by hierarchical level, then, runs 1, 3, 9, 27, 81, 243, and so on. The figure indicates the hierarchy according to this principle. Christaller termed it the *marketing principle* but it is usually referred to as the K=3 network.

Christaller proposed two alternative hierarchies, based on the **transport principle** and the **administrative principle.** According to the transport principle, lower order centers locate at the mid-points of transport routes connecting high order centers and thus bisect the sides of the hexagons rather than locating at the apexes. The progression of numbers of market areas, then runs 1, 4, 16, 64, 256, and so on, or a K=4 network. The administrative principle suggests that each highest order center control a surrounding ring of lower order places, or a K=7 network for a progression of 1, 7, 49, 343, and so on.

It is obvious from the foregoing discussion that Christaller built the hierarchy from the highest order center down. Another student of the theory, August Losch, built the hierarchy from the lowest order center upward, providing a contrasting locational lattice. It has been suggested that the Losch procedure might fit one situation best while the Christaller procedure might fit a different situation best.

The question that remains to be answered is: "Does the pattern fit the real world?" Regarding the progression of market areas, the real world generally offers mixed models depending on population density, disposable income, transport stage at the time of urban development, and so forth. For example, the three or four highest orders might be K=3 and lowest three or four K=4 or K=7, or the entire progression might be a mixture of the three principles. Regarding the hexagonal market areas and center location, researchers are beginning to find the pattern in the real world when modifying influences are removed through map transformation or model simplification. The size, nature, spacing and location of market places (not towns and cities) is fairly accurately described by the central place model.

Cost factors attendent with goods and services modify the model to some extent. That is, certain customers will travel farther to obtain the same or comparable goods and services at a cheaper price. Further, travel may occur even though the total cost, including travel cost, is greater. It has often been demonstrated, however, that people do not know and do not wish to know the real cost of automobile travel. Certain customers may think they are effecting a saving when in actuality they are not.

Effort, exclusive of time and distance required to reach the closest applicable central place, also modifies the model. Certain customers will travel further or for a longer time to reach a place if it is less effort to do so. This might be exemplified by a farmer preferring to travel ten miles or twenty minutes over a paved highway rather than making a three mile, fifteen minute trip over a dirt road, or by a shopper traveling a longer distance in order to utilize a higher probability of finding a parking space.

The socioeconomic status of the customer acts as a modifying factor to the theory. The higher the social or economic status of the customer, the more likely he or she is to trade at higher level centers for all goods and services. Other studies have found that certain rural residents prefer a town of between eight and twelve thousand people, even for grocery purchases alone. Perhaps a customer does not need to be of high economic status to prefer higher level centers for all shopping.

The Central Place Theory is concerned with the totality of markets in any given city or place. The trade area is an aggregate of all the markets. The theory can be applied at a different scale, a scale of individual markets. This scale is termed "the internal business structure" and is concerned with "retail nucleations" and shopping centers. Cities usually contain a central place network to serve their own population. These shopping centers conform, in part, to the central place theory. Lineal thoroughfare or ribbon service districts and specialized areas do not fit the theory, but the regular hierarchy of shopping areas within a city does, presumably, fit the model. Nevertheless, there are differences in the two networks.

The central place model encompasses a seven-part hierarchy, while the intra-city shopping center network is limited to a five part hierarchy. Rural trade areas are deterministic, while shopping center trade areas are probabilistic. That is to say, rural trade areas tend not to overlap. If trade areas are delineated on a map, it is certain (of deterministic) that resident X will utilize shopping place Y or a certain level of goods. Urban shopping center trade areas exhibit considerable overlap, so there is only a chance of probability that resident A will utilize shopping center B. He may decide on center C or D whose trade areas overlap with B center's trade area at his place of residence.

The two networks can be roughly compared and the table below is offered for this purpose.

Table 1

Central Place	Shopping Center	Primary Tenant
Hamlet	small neighborhood or street corner developments	Grocery store or superette
Village	Neighborhood center	Supermarket
Town	Community Center	Junior department or variety store or discount department store
Small City	Regional center	Department store
Regional City		
Regional Metropolis	Super Regional center	Department store
National Metropolis		plus recreation

The reader is urged to approach the table with some caution since there are differences in the two networks which are not evident in the table. For example, the central business district may be the only regional shopping center in a small city, or even in a regional city. It would thus serve both hierarchies. Community shopping centers occur only in higher income areas of a city, while the town bows to no such restriction from the rural country side. The division among junior department store, discount department store, and conventional department store is fuzzy. Many regional cities and regional shopping centers contain a store somewhere between a Woolco or K-Mart and a Marshall Field's: something more complex than "junior" but not a full-line department store. Finally, the metropolitan central business district — the downtown area of a Chicago, a Detroit, or a Philadelphia — is something above and beyond even a super regional shopping center for that population for which it serves as a shopping center.

Functions that are likely to occur in the five levels of urban shopping centers are listed in the Table below. These are generalities and are to be used as a guide only.

Table 2

Shopping Center	Probable Functions
Corner nucleations or small neighborhood	Grocer and/or superette, drugs, hardware.
Neighborhood	All the above — plus supermarket, meat and fish markets, laundry, and dry cleaning pickup, bar, barber and beauty shops, laundromat, restaurant, various repair services.
Community	All the above — plus variety and/or junior department store or discount department store, movie theater, liquor store, stationery and gift store, clothing and shoe stores, furniture store, branch bank, bakery outlet, dairy bar, confectioner, appliances, jewelry, florist, paint and glass, branch post office.
Regional	All of the above — plus department store, stereo store, record store, sports stores, hobby and toy stores, china, drapery and floor covering stores, photographer, book store, cigar stands, furrier, formal rental, professional and financial services, cinemas.
Super-Regional	All the above — plus additional recreation facilities.

Obviously, the list above is not exhaustive and not definitive. Many shopping centers in process of expansion or contraction move up or down between hierarchical levels. Often extent of trade area and function of center do not correspond. Nevertheless, function can be used as a rough guide to hierarchical level.

The central business district (CBD), or downtown area, or a city may serve as a super-regional shopping center for the residents of the city, metropolitan area, and commonly a larger external area. The CBD is usually at the focus of lines of internal urban transport, and is usually the most convenient node for large numbers of customers.

The central business districts of medium-sized and larger cities commonly have a complex internal structure. The highest land values and density of pedestrian traffic are usually associated with what real-estate people call the "hundred percent location" or "hot corner". It is almost always in the heart of the retail portion of the CBD, with department stores adjacent, and specialty shops nearby. Commonly two or more department stores, separated by a short distance, generate considerable pedestrian traffic between or among them, along a lineal axis, the main street of the CBD. Examples are Herald Square and Fifth Avenue in New York, Market Street in San Francisco and Market Street in Philadelphia, State Street in Chicago and Wisconsin Avenue in Milwaukee. Typically, the specialty shops are located along the street, where they can intercept the comparison shoppers walking from one department store to another.

This pattern is replicated in the outlying and suburban shopping centers which were planned and built as unified developments, in which a main axis, open to the sky or covered by roof, connects at least two department stores which are located at opposite ends, serving as "anchors" for the development. Such planned shopping centers, or "malls" consist of islands of retail and service establishments surrounded by a sea of automobile parking.

The typical CBD began either before the era of internal mass transit, when the customers reached the urban core on foot or in horse-powered vehicles from a constricted surrounding area, or they developed when the electric street railway or, in a few larger cities, elevated and subway rapid transit, furnished the principal access. With the shift — except in a few of the very largest cities — to the automobile as the basic local transportation, attempts were made — sometimes moderately successfully — to provide automobile access by creation of parking areas and inner circumferential streets and highways in the fringe areas adjacent to the CBDs, and within convenient distance by walking or use of local shuttle buses. Thus the downtown retail and service establishments could, to some degree, compete with the newer suburban and outlying shopping centers by providing automobile access and parking.

These circumferential streets and express highways are commonly located in the declining "wholesale and light manufacturing" zone which partially or completely encircles the urban core or CBD. Such locations are characterized by older multi-story industrial buildings with high vacancy rates, and by extensive areas of vacant land where demolition of the obsolete buildings took place. Such areas are termed by some geographers and planners as the "frame", "core frame" or transitional zone. "Frame" is used in the same context as "picture frame", and "transitional" zone refers to the area of transition between the closely-spaced buildings of downtown and the lower wider-spaced buildings of outlying residential zones.

The "frame" is an area of mixed land use (i.e., commercial, residential, industrial) while the CBD is more homogenous in character. The frame is geared to vehicular traffic and a flow of goods while the CBD is a pedestrian precinct. The frame is horizontal in character while the CBD is commonly vertical in character. The frame consists of a series of nodes or clusters of uses such as wholesaling, warehousing, light manufacturing, auto sales, loan companies, headquarters of companies, high density residential, and miscellaneous retailing.

With peripheral circulation and parking provided in the "frame" on the fringes of the central business district, it is possible to close one or more streets within the CBD to automobile traffic, and to convert the streets into pedestrian "malls". Although this was common to many European cities after World War II, the first experimental mall of this type in an American city was initiated in Kalamazoo, Michigan, in 1959. During the following two decades, several hundred downtown malls were provided in the United States. Some of the malls are completely closed to vehicular traffic, except for intersecting streets; others, with wide pedestrian walks and narrow, usually two-lane, roadways are restricted to transit Vehicles, including buses and taxicabs. The former are "pedestrian malls", the latter are "transit malls". Both types may be provided with attractive plantings and street furniture, including benches. In some cities the streets, converted into malls, are provided with transparent or translucent cover; and in some cities downtown buildings are interconnected by bridges and upper-level walkways, or by underground plazas, lined with retail establishments, thus providing all-season weather protection.

Downtown malls are not universally successful. The treatment is often cosmetic rather than basic. If the consumer purchasing power is not available either in residential areas in proximity to the central business district or is not conveniently accessible by adequate transportation, no amount of redesign or redevelopment can restore the previous volume of retail sales and service activity.

The thoroughfare service district serves the traveler rather than primarily the nearby residential area. The trade area is a strip along the thoroughfare, as is the commercial development itself. Characteristic establishments provide drive-in one-stop shopping. The thoroughfare service district is deplored by many urban planners, who object to its appearance, its presumed slum-making potential (for residential areas behind the strip) and its contribution to traffic friction. Yet, the thoroughfare service district performs useful services, generates retail sales, and is obviously popular for many customers. The problems and potentials of this type of urban commercial area truly call for further study. Perhaps the thoroughfare service district has been slighted in the literature because it does not conform to the central place theory.

Because of the many constraints to the application of the central place theory to the real world, its critics refuse to refer to it as a "theory". It is true that it does not completely explain the size, nature, spacing, and location of urban places as its author intended. It does, however, explain the nature and size of markets deterministically and the spacing and location of markets in a probabilistic fashion subject to constraints. Whether the student of retailing chooses to refer to Christaller's concept as an idea or hypothesis rather than a theory, it is, at the least, a valuable bridge between *a priori* notions of markets and a descriptive generalization that may fit the real world in a deterministic fashion without constraints.

Delimitation of Trade Areas

It is neither difficult nor time consuming to measure and map a retail trade and service area. All it takes is a little leg work, a little measuring, and a little "plug-in" or "cookbook" statistics. Just follow the step-by-step procedure listed below, whether delineating a trade area for a single retail establishment or for an entire shopping center, the trade and service area of which is the composite of the trade areas of the individual establishments.

Step 1. Collect on-location interviews. Interviewers may stand at the check-out counters or within the malls with permission, or on the public sidewalk without permission, and ask each customer leaving the store his or her residence location. One hundred interviews may be sufficient but two hundred samples has come to be a magic number in marketing circles. One must be careful, though, because trade area extent varies by day-of-the-week and time-of-the-year, so if one wishes to measure the normal or average trade area, one must take one's interviews at mid-week and well away from holidays or special events.

Step 2. Plot residence locations on a map of the city, measure the straight line distance of each to the store, and compute mean and standard deviation for the distances.

$$\text{Mean} = \bar{x} = \frac{x}{N}$$

Mean $= \bar{X}$

Add all the distances together and divide by the number of samples you have taken

$$N$$

$$S\bar{x} = \sqrt{\frac{\frac{x2 - (x)2}{N}}{N - 1}}$$

Standard deviation $= S\bar{x}$

(a) Multiply each distance by itself and add the answers together.

(b) Add all the distances together, multiply the answer by itself, divide by the number of samples you have taken, and subtract the answer from (a).

(c) Divide (b) by one less than the number of samples.

(d) Take the square root of the number remaining.

Step 3. Compute the 95 per cent "one tailed" confidence limits. Confidence limits; 95% = 1.65 $S\bar{x}$

Multiply the standard deviation by 1.65 to obtain the 95% (one-tailed) confidence limits. (The meaning of the term will be explained later.) The table below lists factors necessary to obtain the 95% and others.

Conf. ltd.	Factor
95%	1.65
90%	1.28
75%	.67
25%	.13
10%	.03

Step 4.   Compute the center of gravity of the plotted samples.

Construct a grid on tracing paper with equal cells about one-quarter inch square. Starting at the top-left corner of the grid, number each horizontal line 1-2-3 etc. Then, do the same for the vertical lines. Lay the grid over the map and each dot (representing a residence location) has two co-ordinates. List these in a table e.g.

Sample	X	Y	
1	1	3	
2	17	2	
3	3	15	$\overline{x} = \dfrac{6.6}{N}$ $\overline{y} = \dfrac{5.2}{N}$
4	5	2	
5	7	4	
	33	26	add each column and divide by N

Find the grid intersection represented by the two resulting coordinates and make an X on the map for the center-of-gravity of the residence samples.

Step 5.   Draw a circle, on the map, from the center-of-gravity of the plotted samples with circle radius equal to the 95 per cent confidence limit.

Step 6.   Contract the circle (circumference) where no sample dots appear and extend it to include concentrations of dots beyond the circumference. Outward extensions should balance inward contractions. The original circle area has been retained and the resulting isarithm delineates the trade area, or the area from which 95 per cent of the customers come. The 95 percent confidence limit means: we have confidence, to 95 per cent, that the line does indeed, delineate the trade area; or, to put it another way, 95 per per cent of the customers come from within, 5 per cent from without the isarithm.

Step 7.   Construct a graph depicting the continuum of confidence limits for the trade area. Depict percent on the vertical axis, distance on the horizontal axis. Plot the 95, 90, 75, 25, 10 per cent Confidence limits at points on the graph and connect them with a smooth curved line.

Now you have three items of value: (1) An accurate map with an isarithm delineating a trade area. (2) an index number (95%) that can be used to compare the size of this trade area with any other, and (3) a graph that can be used to estimate the per cent (and thus the number) of customers that come from any given distance within the trade area. It is now also possible to assign demographic characteristics to the customers within the trade area; but, trade area delineation, in itself, is a valuable piece of information.

A trade area is an "amoeba shaped" area on the ground topped by a "distance decay" cone. Lobes of the "amoeba" extend outward along lines of high speed or high-density transport. The cone, in profile, looks enough like the "normal curve" so that inferential statistics can be applied. One-tailed confidence limits are applied because it is easier to work with circle radius than with diameter. That is, we use half the normal curve, then double it. Ninety-five instead of 99% confidence limits are used because studies have shown that, at any given time, about 5 per cent of the customers at a central place are "one time, out-of-area or out of state" people. That is, 95 per cent confidence limits delineate almost all of a trade area.

TRADE AREA

Fig. 8

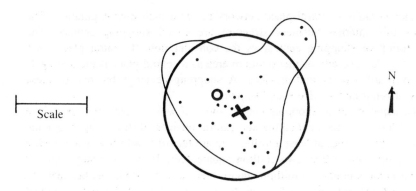

x Center of Gravity

• Sample Dots

° Store Site

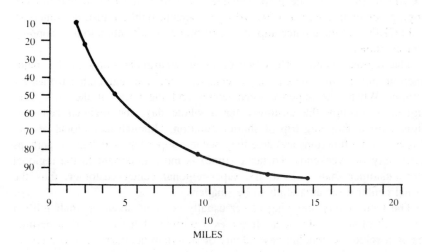

The figures above represent a store trade area as it might appear on a map and a graph indicting ratio of shoppers, at that store, per distance from the store.

Shopping Centers

Cities contain a central place network to serve their own population. The units of this internal business structure are called shopping centers. The consideration of shopping centers vs the consideration of central places is a matter of scale. The city or metropolitan area as a central place is the aggregate of all its retail activity and services. A shopping center is but one of these clusters of retail and service establishments.

The super-regional shopping center, most of which were developed since the mid-1960s, has been called the neo-central business district. Super-regional centers are quite large, at least a million square feet of retail sales space, with a few containing more than two million square feet. However, many regional shopping centers contain a million square feet, so the differences between the two are in trade area size and in the recreation feature of the super-regional center.

The super-regional center of the 1980's does share some characteristics with the CBD of the 1950's, but there are also differences. Similarities include the recreation function, the dependence on metropolitan newspaper advertising, and the cross sectional socio-economic draw. Differences are seen in the number of stores visited per trip (1.3 for the modern shopping center vs 2.5 for the CBD of the 50's), the prepondenance of automobile trips to the modern shopping center in contrast to the 10 to 25 percent public transit customers to the old CBD, and the greater importance of brand identification to the shopping center customer.

The regional center offers two or more department stores as the major attraction and usually lacks a major recreation function, although cinemas are common. Where the super-regional center and the CBD of the 50's were designed to occupy the customer for a whole day, the regional center is designed for a shopping trip of shorter duration, although as regional centers add recreational functions and area they become super-regional centers, perhaps at first only on weekends. Distance (time) is more important to the regional center customer than it is to the super-regional center customer; thus the regional center trade area tends to be smaller.

The Community shopping center usually contains about one-half million square feet of retail sales area. It serves a portion of the city with a definite trade area seldom extending beyond city or suburban boundaries, in contrast to the trade areas of super-regional and regional centers. The community center relies on the junior department store or the variety as the major consumer magnet. It normally does not contain a department store, as do the regional and super-regional centers. Although trade areas of Community centers are rather static year to year, they do expand and contract by day of the week and season of the year. "Image" is very important to the community center customer, and newspaper advertising is of limited value. You won't use the center if it does not fit your perception of your status but if it's "your" center you believe quality is higher and values greater.

The neighborhood center usually contains about 75,000 to 250,000 square feet of retail sales area. The center serves a neighborhood, and urban neighborhoods tend to be socio-economically stratified. The establishments are mainly of the "convenience" type, patronized frequently rather than once a week or less often. Distance (time) regulates trade area size, and thus advertising is of practically no value to the merchants of the center. Trade area sizes vary little day to day, season to season, or year to year.

The corner nucleation serves much the same function as the neighborhood shopping center. In fact the corner nucleation's trade area tends to be about the same size as that of the neighborhood center and may even cover the same area of the city. Nucleations contain anywhere from 25,000 to 100,000 square feet of retail sales area. The superette (15,000 sq. ft., 3 or fewer checkout lanes) is usually the major establishment.

Parking is essential for all shopping centers, inasmuch as almost all customers arrive by auto. However, too many spaces have almost as much negative influence as too few. Too many spaces indicate to the customer that the center is not successful, or perhaps not even open for business. Too few makes it difficult for the potential customer to park. There are methods available for determining the optimum number of spaces for proposed shopping centers.

The Central Business District

The central business district tends to be near the geometric center of the city at the focus lines of transportation, has a large potential captive market in the form of office and industrial workers, and another potential market composed of middle class apartment dwellers nearby, yet in many cities it has lost its primacy as the dominant shopping center, with the outward movement of the middle and upper income population on the one hand and the alternatives of regional and super-regional shopping centers on the other.

One urbanist has suggested that it is not a matter of whether or not we shall have a CBD, but rather how many we shall have. This statement ignors the conversion of the downtowns of small cities from commerce to other uses. There would seem to be very little hope for the continued viability of the downtowns of cities in the 50,000 to 250,000 population size class with regard to commercial land use. The downtowns of some, ever smaller cities (under 50,000 population) have remained viable in many cases because the purchasing power in the trade area has been insufficient to support competing regional and super regional shopping centers. The downtowns of smaller cities have attracted offices, industries that require frequent or rapid face-to-face contact, industries that face deadline delivery schedules, and industries that require a small but skilled labor force. The attraction is, of course, the transport network focusing on the CBD. The commercial segment of the downtowns of these smaller cities has been pared to a size necessary only for service to these functions.

The central business districts of large cities attract the type of function mentioned in the prior paragraph, plus visitors. Visitors, whether from far or near, patronize small retail shops as well as glittering retail palaces. They require food, drink, lodging and entertainment. The commercial sector of many large cities have remained viable in spite of changing conditions.

The downtowns of the United States and the rest of the developed world have performed valuable services for their cities. They have created sales, jobs, and profits and thus brought money into the city that might not otherwise have been there. They have paid a large share of the city's total tax bill. They have concentrated lines of transport that must be relocated to serve shopping centers. They have furnished jobs to many people who cannot afford or are not permitted to live in suburbs or exhurbs. Insofar as these functions decay we all are losers. After all it is the downtown or at least the entertainment districts that characterize cities — Midtown Manhatten, the Loop, the French Quarters — not the residential or industrial districts.

Offices and Hotels

The central business district office industry has continued to be dynamic in many cities in recent years. The downtowns of some small and medium sized cities have become office-oriented, and many new office buildings have risen in the cores of large cities. Yet, during the 1960's and 70's, the office industry expanded faster in the suburbs and exhurbs than it did in the central cities of the United States.

Banking, credit bookers, insurance, investments, accounting, consulting, advertising, and legal services (if the courts are nearby) make up the bulk of core offices. Offices downtown require face-to-face contact. The office industry is extremely labor intensive, and thus rent is a very small part of the total cost of operating an office.

Suburban and exhurban offices are those that specialize in decision making or paper work, and usually do not require face-to-face contact. Other outlying offices are those which cater to a residential clientele, or those near airports for convenient air travel.

Outlying office complexes tend to be near high-cost residential areas or near airports. They include many headquarters companies, professional services, insurance sales, branch banking, and the like.

Hotels were typically located downtown prior to World War II. After the war many outlying motels were built to intercept the automobile traveler until, by the mid 1960's, the number of motel rooms exceeded the number of hotel rooms. The mid-1970's saw a resurgence of downtown hotel building in large cities of the United States. These typically serve the convention and trade-show clientele, although hotels near the larger metropolitan airports often compete successfully for this business.

SELECTED READINGS

Applebaum, William, *Store Location Strategy Cases*, Reading, Mass.: Addison-Wesley Publishing Company, (1968).

Bannon, Michael, "The Office Industry" etc., *Geographical Review* (1975).

Barton, Bonnie, "The Creation of Centrality," *Annals of the Association of American Geographers*, Vol. 68, No. 1, (March 1978) pp. 34-44.

Basile, Ralph J., et. al., *Downtown Development Handbook*. Washington: Urban Land Institute, (1980).

Beavon, K.S.O., *Central Place Theory: A Reinterpretation*, London, Longman (1977).

Berry, Brian J. L., "Ribbon Developments in the Urban Business Pattern," *Annals of the Association of American Geographers*, Vol. 49, No. 2 (June 1959) pp. 145-155.

Berry, Brian J. L. and Garrison, William L., "The Functional Bases of the Central Place Hierarchy" *Economic Geography*, Vol. XXIV, No. 2 (1958) pp. 145.

Berry, Brian J. L. *Geography of Market Centers and Retail Distribution*, Englewood Cliffs, N.J., Prentice-Hall (1967).

Berry, Brian J. L., *Theories of Urban Location*, Association of American Geographers Resource Paper No. 1 (1968).

Christaller, Walter, *Central Places in Southern Germany*, translated by C. Baskin, Englewood Cliffs, N.J.: Prentice-Hall, Inc., (1966).

Clapp, John M., "The Intrametropolitan Location of Office Activities", *Journal of Regional Science*, Vol. 20, No. 3 (August 1980) pp. 387-399.

Cohen, Saul B. and George K. Lewis, "Form and Function in the Geography of Retailing", *Economic Geography*, Vol. 45, No. 1 (January 1967) pp. 1-42.

Corgel, John B. and Harthshorne, Truman A., "Measuring the Impact of Inner City Markets on CBD Retail Sales", *Urban Geography*, Vol. I, No. 1 (Jan.-Mar. 1980).

Daniels, Peter W. (editor), *Spatial Patterns of Office Growth and Location*, New York: John Wiley & Sons, (1979).

Frank, Ronald E., Massy, William F. and Wind, Yoram, *Market Segmentation*, Englewood Cliffs, New Jersey, Prentice-Hall (1972).

Garner, Barry J., *The Internal Structure of Retail Nucleations*, Northwestern University Studies in Geography No. 12 (1966).

Green, Howard L., "The Retailer's Objectives in Choosing a Store Site", *Urban Land*, Vol. 25, No. 6 (June 1966) pp. 1 and 3-6.

Gruen, Victor, *Centers for the Urban Environment: Survival of the Cities*, New York: Van Nostrand Reinhold Company, (1970).

Halpern, Kenneth, *Downtown USA: Urban Design in Nine American Cities*, New York: Whitney Library of Design, (1978).

Hartshorne, Truman A., "Industrial/Office Parks etc." *Journal of Geography*, (1973).

Hayes, Charles R., *The Dispersed City*, Chicago, The University of Chicago Department of Geography Research Paper No. 173 (1976).

Hayes, Charles R. and Bennett, D. Gordon, "The Super-Regional Shopping Center: A New Step in the Market Hierarchy", *Geographical Survey*, Vol. VIII, No. 3 (July 1979) pp. 3-5.

Hayes, Charles R. and Schul, Norman W., "Some Characteristics of Shopping Centers", *The Professional Geographer*, Vol. XVII, No. 6 (1965) pp. 11-14.

Hoyt, Homer, "Classification and Significant Characteristics of Shopping Centers" *The Appraisal Journal*, Vol. 26, No. 2 (April 1958) pp. 214-222.

McKeever, J. Ross, *Business Parks' Office Parks, Plazas and Centers, etc.* Washington, D.C., Technical Bulletin 65, The Urban Institute (1970).

Murphy, Raymond E., *The Central Business District*. Chicago: Aldine, Atherton, Inc., (1972).

Rees, John, "Manufacturing Headquarters in a Post-Industrial Urban Context" *Economic Geography*, Vol. 52, No. 4 (October, 1978) pp. 337-354.

Rubenstein, John M., *Central City Malls*, New York: John Wiley & Sons (1978).

Schuler, Harry J., "A Disaggregate Store-Choice Model of Spatial Decision-Making," *The Professional Geographer*, Vol. 31, No. 2 (May 1979) pp. 146-155.

Smith, Geoggrey C., Shaw, Denis, JLB., and Huckle, Peter R., "Children's Perception of a Downtown Shopping Center", *The Professional Geographer*, Vol. 31, No. 2 (May 1979) pp. 157-164.

Sternlieb, George and Hughes, James W., *Shopping Centers USA*, Piscataway, N.J. Center for Urban Policy Research, Rutgers University (1981).

Tinkler, Keith, "A Co-ordinate System for Studying Interactions in the Primary, Christaller Lattice," *The Professional Geographer*, Vol. 30, No. 2 (May 1978) pp. 135-139.

United States Department of Commerce, *Market Center Shifts*, Washington, D.C. (1978).

Urban Land Institute, *Parking Requirements for Shopping Centers*, Technical Bulletin 53, Washington, D.C. (1965).

Weiss, Shirley R., *The Central Business District in Transition*, Chapel Hill. N.C., City and Regional Planning Studies No. 1, (1957).

CHAPTER SEVEN

Industrial Land Use

Economic Base

The employment or livelihood structure of a city, metropolitan area, region, state, or nation is termed its "economic base". Cities require income in order to function. The sources of income constitute their economic base. The economic base of a city explains why it exists, or at least what makes it "tick". Measures of economic base are also used to explain past growth and to forecast future growth. Economic base statistics are also used by chambers of commerce and industrial development groups as sales tools for solicitation of industry. Economic base information is also used as input for traffic forecasting.

If one were to construct a table of all industry in a city or metropolitan area, classified according to employment one would have the beginning of a simple economic base study. Of course the table would have to be analyzed to be meaningful, but an experienced analyst could describe the employment sector of the city quite well from the table. The study would be only as good as the analyst and would not be directly comparable to economic base analyses from other cities because the methods and levels of analysis would vary with each analyst. The study would not lend itself well to prediction, but a substantial portion of the needed data would be readily available from the census and such a study would be relatively easy to do.

The Economic Base Hypothesis (often called the Basic/Non-basic hypothesis — B/N for short) is a commonly used method for describing the economic or employment sector of a city. The Economic Base Hypothesis assumes that city growth and income level are tied to the supplying of goods and services to people and organizations outside the city. The basic (B) sector is comprised of all goods and services produced for export beyond the city. The non-basic (N) sector is comprised of all goods and services produced for local consumption. There are several ways to measure the basic/non-basic activities.

An early suggestion for logically separating the basic from the non-basic activity of a city was offered by Homer Hoyt in 1939. The method employs a simple ratio statement. If for example, one wishes to separate the basic steel workers of metropolitan Chicago from the non-basic steel workers of the same area, it is necessary only to substitute numbers from the census in the following formula and cross-multiply. Steel workers of the U.S.: Labor force of the U.S.:: steel workers of metropolitan Chicago: Labor force of metropolitan Chicago. The excess represents basic workers. All sectors of the labor force are computed in this manner to determine the B/N ratio of the city. The method assumes that per capita consumption and per capita productivity are the same throughout the nation. This, of course, is not true. The method also assumes that all cities and metropolitan areas supply the local demand first. This, also, is not entirely true. On the other hand, data are available from the census, computation is easy, results are easily understood and directly comparable city to city. Nevertheless, because of the disadvantages of the method, it is used in only a few cities, and then only for very crude approximations.

The interview method is the method employed in most cities for determining B/N ratio. Interviewers ask each employer, or a carefully selected stratified sample of employers in a city, what per cent of his goods or service he sells or provides locally vs. the per cent exported from the city. The interviewer then determines the number of workers employed by each firm. The basic and non-basic components of the goods or service produced by the company are assigned to employees. For example, for a firm employing one hundred people and selling forty per cent of the product locally, forty workers could be assigned to the non-basic sector, sixty to the basic sector. This method is probably the most accurate of the several mentioned. It is directly comparable, city to city, it is easy to do and easy to understand. However, it requires field work which is both time-consuming and expensive. Nevertheless the method is widely employed for determining the basic-nonbasic ratio of cities and metropolitan areas.

The minimum or average requirements technique is a slightly different method. The procedure is as follows: (1), Assign the cities or metropolitan areas of the country to size groups, (2), Assign all employment or income to certain census categories, (3), Determine the city or metropolitan area in each group with the smallest per cent of employment or income in each category. This is defined as the minimum per cent of employment or income, in the category, that a city or metropolitan area in a particular size group can have, and it becomes the non-basic component. This method shares the advantages and disadvantages of the proportionate formula method with two exceptions. An additional disadvantage is the assumption that all but one city or area in each size group exports, in the category in question, and none imports. This is clearly not true. However, an additional advantage is that computation is less time consuming for this than for the proportional formula method.

A variation of the minimum requirements method is the average requirements method, which uses the average percentage of each category of employment or income to total employment or income.

Although the B/N ratio has been widely used for several purposes, it has also been widely criticized. For example, although it would seem that the B/N ratio would be directly comparable, city to city, if computed by the same method, it is not, because of the difficulty of city delineation. It makes a great difference to the ratio where the line is drawn to designate "city", because establishments are included or excluded by boundary placement. Further, although the concept is simple, it is not always easy to decide just what is basic and what is non-basic. The sharpest criticism though, is that the larger the city the higher the ratio of non-basic workers. This is so because a large city or metropolitan area tends to constitute a major portion of its own market and needs less export to prosper. Because of the criticism of the B/N hypothesis, other methods of describing or predicting economic or total urban growth have been suggested.

A widely used method for predicting economic or population growth of a city is the stochastic or probabilistic model. Although there are many such models, they all assume that economic and population growth are closely linked but that growth takes place only through new investment. That is, current investment merely maintains population or economy. Some of these stochastic models show a very close fit when used experimentally to predict known growth years.

The input/output model has also been suggested as an alternative to the B/N hypothesis. This model analyzes economic base through a series of in-out matrices. In order to run such a model, all inputs and outputs to or from a city, metropolitan area, or sector of a city must be reduced to comparable figures. This amount to reducing them to coefficients. The amount of input per unit of output can be computed to indicate the effect of industrial increase or decrease on everything else in the economy. This method requires very little value judgement and is obviously a potential predictive tool. Although the input/output method is commonly applied in studies of national economies, the stupendous mass of data which is required, much of which is unavailable for subnational areas, makes the method impracticable for use in regional, metropolitan and city economic base studies.

The entire concept of urban economic base analysis has been criticized by many scholars, though it has been and continues to be a popular method for describing a city or metropolitan area and for forecasting urban growth. Proponents of the concept claim the theory is sound and point to incorrect or incomplete data or methodology when the system does not describe or predict well. Opponents of the concept claim that cities and metropolitan areas are too closely tied to each other and to surrounding regions to be subject to individual analysis. These scholars suggest that the interaction of an entire "city region" must be analyzed in order to even describe, let alone forecast, city livelihood and growth.

Proponents of the "city region" theory point out that growth rates are completely unpredictable for small cities. Some cities with populations of less than a quarter of a million show very low growth rates and some show very high growth rates. Further, growth rates fluctuate for cities in this size class over time. These people point out that cities in the medium size class (250,000 - 2 million) though stabilizing in growth, are not yet subject to accurate growth prediction.

City region theorists concede that the growth rates of small cities may well depend on the ratio of the basic vs. non-basic components of the city. They believe that economic base is easily influenced in cities within this size class because one large industrial or commercial establishment can have great influence on the livelihood structure of a small city. Since it is often possible to solicit, successfully, one or two large industrial plants, economic base will never be stable, and growth or decline never predictable.

Many medium-sized cities depend less for growth of the basic sector since their local market is larger than is the local market for small cities. Growth of these medium sized cities depends on access to local, regional, and national markets and on inertia.

Large cities depend very little on the basic sector of the economy. Localization and inertia plus local, regional, national, and international market access determine growth for these largest cities. In many instances a limited number of specialized nonubiquitous activities constitute the basic component of the economy, i.e. automobiles in Detroit, etc.

All cities in the nation can be arranged within regions in a hierarchy of size and importance. The largest city in a region can be regarded as the regional economic capital, and the hierarchy of smaller cities the sub-nodes. Flows of people, goods, information, and ideas tend to go up the hierarchy of urban nodes toward the regional capitals. Thus, regional capitals constantly gain at the expense of the sub-nodes. In time, the best qualified people work and live in regional capitals, leaving the smaller centers relatively backward. Regional capitals, then, tend to adopt innovation first: the smaller centers only later, if at all. The early adoption of innovation can have an important effect on income and on growth.

It is necessary only to consider the diffusion of television broadcasting within the United States to demonstrate the importance of the early adoption of innovation. Television broadcasting originated in the largest cities of the United States. In its early days, executives, technicians, and talent were paid very high salaries and wages. When one industry within a city pays high wages and salaries there is a tendency for all industry to increase wages and salaries in order to hold their skilled employees. This principle is called "intra-area wage roll-out" and is defined as the tendency for all wages to "roll-out" (i.e. be the same) within an area or region. Since wages and salaries tend to be high within the large city, qualified people tend to migrate to that city. By the time television broadcasting diffused down the size hierarchy of cities, in two or three waves, wages and salaries decreased. A city with two hundred thousand people does not pay television personnel as much as does a city with several million people because revenues are not as large and because the television employees do not need to be as skilled as those in the very large market. Further, by the time television broadcasting reaches the smaller cities there are many more trained people competing for the available jobs. The economic impact of the innovation of television broadcasting, then, is not as great on the smaller city as it was on the larger city.

If the city region hypothesis is accepted, the logical question is: why do some small cities exhibit very high growth rates? City region proponents believe that it is because it does not require much of a change in the basic sector of a small city to change the whole economic base for the city. This can be altered through successful industrial solicitation, but the city region proponents point out other means of change for the basic sector of small cities in the United States.

Many of the small cities in the United States are located on the coastal periphery. Much of the coastline of the United States is in the Southern part of the country. These cities, then, have an opportunity to capitalize on resort and retirement potential. This, in effect, is the export of amenities. Further, the longevity committee system in Congress encourages the flow of government capital to, at least, the Southeastern portion of the country. This impact enhances the potential for growth in these small cities.

The economic base hypothesis and the city region hypothesis are alternate means of explaining and/or predicting city growth. A third view of city growth through the economic sector might be called the "one region" hypothesis. This view holds that the United States is becoming a single large region. Proponents of this view look at retail and wholesale trade, migration, bank deposits, etc. and claim that the ten (or so) very largest metropolitan areas in the country are beginning to draw flows of all kinds from all over the country, not just from a region.

This is however, not necessarily reflected in sustained population growth of the largest central cities and even metropolitan areas, many of which are losing population, due in part to improvements in communication and the ubiquity of modern transportation.

These largest metropolitan areas, then, are growing at the expense of all other such areas in the nation according to the hypothesis. The exceptions to this are the smaller cities high in amenity value and the smaller cities that have unusual access to government capital. These smaller cities will continue to grow, along with the very largest cities, because of resort, retirement, and government spending.

The economy of cities is certainly an important, perhaps the most important, reason for city growth. It should be borne in mind, however, that there are other reasons for the existence of cities and other reasons for city growth. No social scientist should become over-impressed with the importance of the economy to a city. A city is best defined in terms of its people, and people are influenced by social and cultural factors as well as economic factors.

Many small cities, suburbs, exhurbs, and counter-urbanized non-urban places have employed economic base concepts to promote a low-or no-grow policy. As more and more artificial restrictions to in-migration are struck down by the courts (although not all such ordinances are denied) and as more and more planning lawyers agree that the right to mobility was so well established by the time the United States constitution was written that no separate amendment was necessary, industrial non-solicitation emerges as a viable means to limit in-migration. No tax breaks, poor access roads, no water and sewer, etc. will discourage some industrial re-location and; "no jobs-no people".

Urban Industry

A city provides services for its hinterland and for its own people. These services include processing — manufacturing, wholesaling, warehousing, and transportation — the industrial component.

There are agglomerating or urbanizing forces and counter-urbanizing forces. In spite of a strong trend in the United States and in the rest of the developed world for counter-urbanization there are strong forces that attract industry into a city or metropolitan area.

Transport-oriented industries are those for which transportation represents a major cost component of the finished product. Certain transport-oriented industries are attracted to the source of raw materials, others to the market. The latter are termed market-oriented transport-oriented industries.

Market-oriented, transport-oriented industries are those whose products cost more to transport than do the raw materials, because of added bulk or weight. Machinery manufacturing is an example of this. The assembled machine is considerably more bulky than are the assembly components, which can often be nested for shipment. The components, however, are bulkier than the metal required to fabricate them, so even component manufacturing would be market-oriented. Machinery manufacturing also adds weight to the finished product through fasteners and welds.

Market-oriented, transport-oriented industries are also those which receive homogenous raw material but which ship complex finished products. The petroleum refining industry is an example of this.

Market-oriented, transport-oriented industries are also those which require frequent or rapid customer contact. Job printing is an example of this, as is film making or still photography, for the advertising business. It is simply too costly and inconvenient to transport people and equipment to the market frequently or at a moment's notice. There is also a factor operating in any industry in which customer contacts are sensitive, which tends to keep that industry close to the market. This factor might be termed "ivory tower bias". Management often feels more secure against competition if customers are close so that contact can be frequent and informal.

Linkage or localization is another very important industrial location factor, which tends to attract and retain manufacturing in or near cities. This is because of the economies of agglomeration. There are many reasons for those cost economies. Some are listed in the following paragraphs:

1. There is a large pool of skilled labor in or near large cities. Advertising, public relations, consulting, banking, publishing, design, and the like are services usually available predominantly in or near large cities.

2. Municipal utilities and services become adapted to needs of a particular manufacturing industry, and the public pays part of the cost.

3. Certain manufacturing industries can maintain common inventories which result in a saving. Subvision of operation can also result in economies; these are best achieved in many instances where many similar industries locate in proximity.

4. The reputation of a locality may be an important marketing aid and constitute an attraction for industry. For example, Milwaukee is known for beer, New York for its clothing styles, etc. On the other hand, technological and other changes may eventually reduce the significance of reputation and an attractive force.

5. Large cities not only represent a large market in themselves but often provide better access to the national and international markets, in large part because of the roles of large cities as nodes of transportation and communication.

In fact, new industry often starts in a city to take advantage of one or more of the factors listed above, then moves in search of cheaper or less organized labor when design, process, and marketing become standardized.

Inertia can also be an important factor in industrial localization. Inertia represents the failure of a manufacturer to move even though the original location factors have disappeared. Inertia may be for economic or social reasons and applies to many plants and industrial agglomerations throughout the nation. Inertia may keep a manufacturing plant in a particular city. The plant might have moved except for inertia.

Ubiquitous manufacturing industries are those that occur in or near all cities. Those manufacturers have a highly perishable or very low value product. Newspaper publishing and bread baking are examples of the former: bricks and cement are examples of the latter. Milk processing is also an example of ubiquitous manufacturing, since a milk-shed surrounds every large city in the United States.

Dovetailing is the process whereby a supplier located his plant in proximity to one or more large customers. The most obvious examples of dovetailing in the United States are the several can plants abutting food or beverage packers. For this particular dovetailing situation the tin can conveyor belt is extended through a common wall so the finished cans are never touched before they are filled with product.

Symbiosis is the process whereby a manufacturing establishment is located in proximity to the source of a by-product used in the manufacturing process. The by-product may be labor or material. The knitting industry in High Point, North Carolina was started in order to utilize the wives of furniture manufacturing workers as an inexpensive but trainable labor force. A particular cosmetic manufacturer in the Chicago area uses the remnants of tin plated steel sheets (from which bottle caps have been stamped) as a base for certain cosmetics.

Ports represent opportunities to process materials where transfers among carriers takes place. Since a ship can carry more cargo than a train and a truck, the bulk of the cargo shipment must be broken anyway, and processing takes place. More important, though, is the fact that all cargo passing through the port must pay additional terminal cost at the point of origin. This, in effect, reduces the terminal cost to zero for manufacturers located in the port city, because manufacturers located elsewhere, shipping through the port, must pay an additional terminal cost at the point of origin. Thus transportation nodes and urbanization go hand in hand.

All this leads to a skilled, sophisticated, specialized, but diversified urban population with high wages, high salaries, and high disposable income.

The factors mentioned in the prior paragraphs tend to locate industry in or near a city, but where in a city? Four typical locations can be generalized; the core, the frame, linear along the rail lines, and peripheral.

The core or central business district is near the center of the city at the focus of the lines of transportation. This district, of course, contains many other functions, but as an industrial district tends to harbor light industry. Core industry is often the type requiring frequent face-to-face contact (e.g. publishing) and locates here because of the focus of transportation lines. Also, small industries that need a small, but highly skilled labor force locate here for the same reason. Further, industries that must make speedy or deadline deliveries are located here, again to take advantage of the focus of lines of transport. With the development of good highways and trucking and the peripheral movement of port terminals, airports, railroad freight yards and truck terminals, many industries which formerly were characteristic of central locations are now more typically located near the edges of cities or beyond.

The "frame" is the area surrounding the core. The frame is also called the "transitional zone" indicating the transition or change from the tall buildings of downtown to the lower buildings of the rest of the city. The frame is in the same relative location as the core and contains some of the same types of industry as the core, but also often contains many wholesaling firms, though the items wholesaled tend to be small or light. The disadvantage of the frame vs. the core is that it is a little farther from the transport focal point, but the advantage is often in cheaper rent because of location and older buildings. In fact, some of this has come about because of the outward migration of industry formerly located in the frame. These older buildings are often subdivided into small areas renting relatively inexpensively, and thus, is a good place for a new firm to start. However, once successful, the establishment often joins the exodus. In many cities, the frame is characterized by high vacancy rates in the old multi-story buildings and much vacant land which, at one time, constituted the sites of freight terminals and industries which no longer needed to be centrally located.

Railroads extending outward from the center of the city usually have considerable industry along their rights-of-way. This is commonly the result of inertia: industry that once shipped and received by rail no longer does so, but has not relocated. However, such locations provide cheaper land and larger available blocks of it so larger and heavier industry tends to locate there. Such locations may be attractive for wholesaling, especially for larger and heavier items. Even if an industry uses trucks exclusively, or ships by "piggy-back", in which inter-city movement is by truck semi-trailers or containers on railroad flatcars, a location here avoids the congestion of the city center. In fact, there are still many truck terminals in such locations, though most have moved farther out. Finally, the city is often not so "picky" about noise or pollution in these locations, so some industries that might be considered "noxious" also locate there.

The periphery and beyond is the newest and largest industrial zone. Land is cheapest and available in the largest blocks there so many industries prefer this type of location. Much industry has moved here from closer-in, but many establishments have relocated from places other than the nearest central city, or have originated in the urban periphery. Because of land availability, production lines are often horizontal rather than the vertical style usually necessary closer to the city center. Industry in a peripheral location is often clustered into so-called industrial parks.

Industrial Counter-urbanization

Industry has located or relocated at some distance from cities, people have followed the jobs, and commerce has followed the people. Although suburbanization or outward movement has always occured, the exodus became so dramatic after World War II that it was given a new name: counter-urbanization. The difference between suburbanization and counter-urbanization is in the numbers moving and the distance of the moves, although counter-urbanization is defined as movement from within to outside metropolitan boundaries.

In order to understand industrial counter-urbanization we must take a look at the 19th century industrial city and compare it to the modern contemporary city.

The 19th century city was almost completely core-dominated. Most commercial and industrial establishments were in or near the city center. Most employment was centered, in order to shop for anything but convenience items it was necessary to travel downtown. Why was this so? To understand we must consider the major factors of production and the transport systems of the time.

Capital may or may not be completely mobile within the borders of a country, as many economists suggest, but it surely is mobile within a metropolitan area. That is, it should cost no more to borrow money whether a plant is inside or outside metropolitan boundaries.

Rent (land cost), as has already been pointed out, declines with distance from the city center.

Labor costs should be less outward from the city center. To consider this statement, imagine you owned a manufacturing operation in a downtown location that employed just one other person. If you offered to relocate your plant to your employee's neighborhood he might well accept a wage reduction amounting to the cost of his daily transportation to and from work. He might even accept a further wage reduction for the added convenience and time saving from living closer to work. But, at any rate, even if you did not save money it should amount to no more in labor cost to move your plant outward.

Capital should have cost no more in the 19th century with an outward industrial move, rent should have cost less, and labor less or at least no more. Why then was the 19th century city core dominated? The answer lies in the transportation systems of the time.

The principal inter-urban transporter of people in the 19th century was the railroad. Rail was quite an efficient transporter mode, exhibiting good economy of scale. The major inter-urban transporter of goods in the 19th century was also rail. Rail was, and is, an efficient mover of goods, especially of low value goods over relatively long distances.

The intra-urban transporter of people in the late 19th century and early 20th century was rail (we called them street cars). The street railway was an efficient mover of people. The 19th century intra-urban goods was, however, the horse and wagon. The horse-drawn wagon was an inefficient goods mover — more like 10th century than 19th century technology.

The great cost of moving goods vs. moving people within the 19th century city kept it core-dominated inasmuch as it was considerably cheaper to bring the people to the goods rather than vice-versa. The introduction and increasing use of the motor truck acted to change the relative cost of intra-urban transport of people vs. goods and released industry from the city center.

The motor truck came into general use after World War I, and each technological innovation has increased its efficiency as an intra-urban mover of goods until it drove the horse from the city streets. The glue holding the core-dominated American city together has dissolved.

Industry has to a large degree counter-urbanized, the people have followed the jobs, and commerce has followed the people. But where and in which direction?

Many industrial establishments have moved beyond upper-middle and high cost residential neighborhoods and suburbs. As automation and the machine, together with electronic communication and data transmission have taken over more and more tasks, the required skill levels are continually being up-graded. Industry near high cost residential areas has a better chance of filling positions requiring high skills than does industry located near low cost residential areas.

It would seem that industry and industrial employees enjoy the best of both worlds. Work is performed in a pastoral environment, and living can be either urban or rural with a short journey in either direction. Of course the city misses the taxes no longer paid by counter-urbanized industry but all is not lost even here. Industry still buys many professional, commercial, and personal services in the city.

It should be re-emphasized that, although the truck has facilitated the outward movement of industry, the automobile has permitted the people to follow. Most counter-urbanized people work in counter-urbanized jobs, shop in counter-urbanized centers, play in counter-urbanized spaces and move in private automobiles. Thus, the cores of cities are less attractive to industrial and commercial establishments, except in certain specialized instances, and cities increasingly tend to diffuse and to coalesce into dispersed, multi-nucleated patterns, held together by increasingly effective transportation and communication.

SELECTED READINGS

Alexander, John W., "The Basic-Non Basic Concept of Urban Economic Functions", *Economic Geography*, Vol. 30, No. 3 (1954) pp. 246.

Barber, Gerald M., "Locating Employment Growth in Urban Areas to Minimize Travel Time," *The Professional Geographer*, Vol. 30 No. 2 (May 1978) pp. 149-155.

Bennett, Marshall, "Industrial Parks: Big Business in the Suburbs," *Britannica Book of the Year 1964*. Chicago: Encyclopedia Britannica, Inc., (1964), pp. 433-434.

Blumenfield, Hans, "The Economic Base of the Metropolis," *Journal of the American Institute of Planners*, Vol. 21, No. 4 (1955).

Borchert, John R., "America's Changing Metropolitan Regions," in Hart, John Fraser, ed. *Regions of the United States*, New York, Harper and Row (1972).

Braschler, Curtis H., "Importance of Manufacturing in Areas Economic Growth," *Land Economics*, Vol. XLVII (Feb. 1971), pp. 109-111.

Clark, Gordon L., "The Employment Relation and Spatial Division of Labor: A Hypothesis," *Annals of the Association of American Geographers*, Vol. 71, No. 3 (Sept. 1981) pp. 412-424.

Clark, W.A.V. and Burt, James E., "The Impact of Workplace on Residential Relocation," *Annals of the Association of American Geographers*, Vol. 70, No. 1, (March 1980) pp. 59-67.

Dorf, Ronald J., and M. Jarvin Emerson, "Determinants of Manufacturing Plant Location For Non-Metropolitan Communities in the West North Central Region of the U.S.," *Journal of Regional Sciences*, Vol. 18, No. 1 (April 1978), pp. 109-120.

Hayes, Charles R. and Schul, Norman W., "Why do Manufacturers Locate in the Southern Piedmont?" *Land Economics*, Vol. XLIV, No. 1, (Feb. 1968), pp. 117-121.

Hoover, Edgar M., *The Location of Economic Activity*, New York, McGraw Hill (1948).

Hoyt, Homer, *The Economic Status of the New York Metropolitan Region in 1944*. New York: Regional Plan Association, 1944.

Industrial Development Handbook. Washington: Urban Land Institute, (1975).

Leinbach, Thomas R., "Location Trends in Nonmetropolitan Industrial Growth et. al.," *The Professional Geographer*, Vol. 30, No. 1 (Feb. 1978) pp. 30-36.

Livingston, Lawrence, Jr., "Business and Industrial Development," Chapt. 9 of: Frank S. So., *et. al.* (editors), *The Practice of Local Government Planning*, Washington: International City Management Association, (1979), pp. 246-272.

Mayer, Harold M., "Centex Industrial Park: An Organized Industrial District," in Thoman, Richard C. and Patton, Donald J., *Focus on Geographic Activity*, New York, McGraw-Hill (1964) pp. 135-145.

Mayer, Harold M., "Making a Living in Cities: The Urban Economic Base," *Journal of Geography*, Vol. 68, No. 2 (Feb. 1969), pp. 70-87.

Mayer, Harold M., "Planning for Industry and Commerce," Chap. 5 of: William H. Claire (editor), *Handbook on Urban Planning*, New York: Van Nostrand Reinhold Company, (1973), pp. 113-174.

Mayer, Harold M., "Urban Nodality and the Economic Base," *Journal of the American Institute of Planners*, Vol. 20, No. 3 (Summer 1954), pp. 117-121.

Moses, Leon N. and Williamson, Harold F., "Factor Prices, Transport Technology and the Urban Economy" Economics Research Center Report (Evanston, Ill.) Northwestern University, (1965).

Ottensmann, John R., "Changes in Accessibility to Employment in an Urban Area: Milwaukee," 1927-1963, *Professional Geographer*, Vol. 32, No. 4, (Nov. 1980) pp. 421-430.

Pred, Allen R., "The Intrametropolitan Location of American Manufacturing" *Annals of the Association of American Geographers*, Vol. 54, No. (1964) pp. 165-180.

Pred, Allen R., *Major Job-Providing Organizations and Systems of Cities*, Washington, D.C., Association of American Geographers, Research Paper No. 27 (1974).

Smith, David M., *Industrial Location*, New York, John Wiley & Sons (1971), (1981).

Schul, Norman W. and Hayes, Charles R., "Intra-Urban Manufacturing Land Use Patterns et. al., *Southeastern Geographers*, Vol. VIII (1968), pp. 39-45.

Ullman, Edward and Dacey, Michael, "The Minimum Requirements Approach to the Urban Economic Base," *The Regional Science Association Papers and Proceedings*, Vol. 6 (1960).

Wrigley, Robert L., Jr., "Organized Industrial Districts with Special Reference to the Chicago Area," *Journal of Land and Public Utility Economics*, Vol. 23 (1947), pp. 180-198.

Yaseen, Leonard C., *Plant Location*, New York: American Research Council, (1965), 226 pp.

CHAPTER EIGHT

Public and Institutional Land Uses

Public and institutional land uses constitute a miscellaneous category of land uses which vary greatly in characteristics and extent, having in common only the attribute that they serve public needs, and, in general, that their operations are not for private profit. Because of the great variety of such land uses it is virtually impossible to generalize about them. Public ownership may be by federal, state, county or local governments, or by special-purpose *ad hoc* governments and public agencies which exist to perform certain functions such as sewage collection, treatment, and disposal, water supply, flood control, drainage, recreation, *ad infinitum*. For several decades such special-function governments have been proliferating both in variety and in numbers; the only such type of special-purpose governmental body which has been decreasing in numbers is the school district, especially in rural and suburban areas, because consolidation of small school districts achieves the economy of scale which makes possible more adequate facilities and services to the students.

In the thirty-five years between 1942 and 1977, the number of local governments in the United States declined from 155 thousand to 80 thousand. Nearly all the decline was accounted for by reduction in the number of school districts; from nearly 109 thousand to slightly over 15 thousand during the period. Meanwhile special districts other than school districts increased from about 8.3 thousand to nearly 26 thousand.

In addition to governmental land uses, extensive areas of land are devoted to use by private non-profit organizations which perform public service functions. These include private schools, colleges and universities, private hospitals and other health facilities, and non-profit recreational and general institutions such as camps, YMCAs. *etc.* One of the most common types of institutional land users is the religious institution: churches, synagogues, and ancillary facilities owned or operated by religious institutions for educational, social service and recreational purposes.

Because of the great variety of public and institutional land users it is not possible to generalize relative to the proportions of the land areas of cities and metropolitan regions devoted to such uses; it may vary from well under ten percent to as much as half or more.

Some public land uses may be unique or sporadic in location. Not every city or metropolitan area, for example, has a large military base, nor do they all have large university campuses. On the other hand, certain public land uses are virtually ubiquitous; fire and police stations serve every urban area, and most have public systems of water supply and sewage collection and treatment.

In this chapter some of the more common types of public and institutional land uses are considered.

Health and Medical Services and Land Use

Health and medical services constitute a group of functions which occupy land in urban areas, and which in recent years have received increasing attention by geographers and planners.

These services, and the facilities required to perform them, may be divided into two general categories: preventive services and remedial services, although in some instances they occupy common facilities.

In a general sense, preventive services relate to general community health. In turn, environmental conditions are major determinants of community health, and the facilities relating to the maintenance and improvement of the environment can be considered as health facilities. They include, among others: water supply, treatment and distribution systems; sewage collection, treatment and disposal systems, facilities for the disposal of solid wastes, parks, forest preserves and other public open spaces whether used for recreation or not, and facilities for the prevention or reduction of natural hazards. In addition, preventive facilities include health clinics, and facilities within which programs of public health education are operated.

Remedial facilities include offices of physicians and other health professionals. These are usually included as commercial land uses unless they are publicly-operated or not-for-profit clinics, hospitals and other institutions devoted to medical and dental practice under public or institutional auspices.

As for many other facilities for supplying goods and services in urban areas, the location of medical facilities, and consequently the land uses occupied by such facilities, tend to be spatially arranged in accordance with the classical central place hierarchical model. The more specialized the service, the less ubiquitous the facilities and the more extensive the service area. General medical practitioners are located closer to the area from which their patients are derived than are medical specialists and general hospitals are more numerous than those with a specialization.

There are many difficulties in the application of the central place model to the location of facilities for the delivery of health care in urban areas. The demand is not completely correlated with the spatial distribution of the population, nor are the facilities always located where the demand is greatest. Recent planning has emphasized better siting of available medical services in the lower-income areas of cities. Among the factors in the location, accessibility, and use of health care facilities are the level and type of care, the ability to pay, demographic and cultural differences, and accessibility in terms of distance and transportation facilities.

A number of federal health care programs during the 1960s were devoted to improving access to health care services by reducing cost constraints (i.e. Medicare and Medicaid). Subsequently, additional emphasis in public programs at the federal, state and local levels was placed upon reduction of spatial constraints, by improving physical accessibility, both by reducing travel distances and reducing travel time. Not only do lower-income persons have less ability to pay for health care, they also have less ability to travel to the locations where the services are available. At the same time, the demand per capita, because of higher morbidity rates, is greater in the poorer areas of cities. Consequently, the discrepancies between the demand for and the supply of both preventive and remedial medical services is greatest in these poorer areas.

Medical services may, in general, be divided into two categories: (1) services by physicians in both individual and group practice, and (2) hospital services.

Primary medical care is mainly in the offices of physicians. About three out of every four patient visits take place in physicians' offices, the remainder being divided into the outpatient departments and emergency rooms of hospitals, offices of prepaid medical practices, neighborhood health centers, and free clinics.

Individual and group practice offices of physicians are generally located in commercial districts. Many of the planned community and regional shopping centers contain buildings predominantly occupied by medical and dental practitioners, either within the centers themselves or nearby. Central business districts also contain large numbers of medical and dental offices and laboratories. Over three-fourths of the physicians are specialists because the proportion of general practitioners has steadily decreased. In general, the narrower the specialty, the larger the area from which patients come. Thus the central areas of cities tend to contain highly specialized medical practitioners.

On the other hand, with the decline of urban mass transit and the general dependence upon the automobile, many medical specialists tend to locate in or near the more affluent peripheral or suburban areas, where a larger proportion of patients can afford the higher fees for specialized services. A suburban phenomenon of recent years has been the proliferation of clusters of office buildings, both in central business districts and in suburban areas, with concentrations of medical and dental specialists. With such concentrations, there is a demand for laboratory services and pharmacies nearby. In many instances, individual buildings may be nearly self-contained medical centers containing both practitioners and auxiliary service establishments.

The two-fold trend toward downtown concentrations and suburban locations has reduced the availability of medical services in many portions of the lower-income "inner-city" neighborhoods. In some instances, hospitals which formerly served more affluent clientele, now have only lower-income residents to serve. Consequently these hospitals must be supported primarily by Medicare and Medicaid payments. Typically, older urban areas have surplus hospital capacity, as the result of over-building, in many instances with federal funds under the Hill-Burton Act. At the same time new hospitals were built in peripheral areas. Vacant redundant former hospital buildings are familiar sights in the older portions of many cities. Many physicians have also deserted such areas.

There tends to be a rough correlation between the sizes of hospitals and the number and character of the specialized services which they provide. Within or on the fringes of central business districts, or in locations within the "inner-city", several hospitals and associated institutions may cluster, in order to share some externalities. These include laboratory services, and certain specialized equipment and practices which may not be economically practicable for an individual hospital to provide. In some of the larger clusters, residential facilities may be available for physicians and staff, as well as hotel and motel facilities for the patients and relatives of patients served by the nearby hospitals. In terms of the central place hierarchy, such clusters, as well as a relatively few individual very large hospitals, may be regarded as "first order" central places, drawing their patronage from the entire metropolitan area, and, in some instances, from the entire nation; a few attract patients from abroad for highly specialized services.

Such concentrations of medical facilities commonly constitute conspicuous visual nodes in inner city areas. Because of high land values, they may be housed in multiple-story buildings, many of them skyscrapers looming high above their surroundings. Commonly, institutions in such locations have difficulty recruiting staff, medical personnel, and even patients because of the physical and social deterioration of the surroundings and the high crime rates. In particular, middle-class and affluent private patients are reluctant to travel through the older neighborhoods. In a number of noteworthy instances, hospitals, individually or in groups, have been instrumental in initiating and executing (both with their own and with public funds) substantial urban redevelopment and renewal programs in their vicinities, serving as nodes for even more extensive urban rebuilding. On the other hand, urban redevelopment has involved the uprooting of many poor families as the institutions themselves as well as associated housing and other land uses spread. To minimize such social trauma, many of the redeveloped inner city medical institutions have gone high-rise, resulting in extremely high-density land use.

There is an acute need for metropolitan and regional planning of medical and health facilities and services, not only to minimize duplication and overlap but also to provide the needed services, and access to them, both economically and spatially. The difficulty is compounded by the fact that such facilities and services are partly provided by government, at all levels from federal to local, and partly by private organizations both non-profit and proprietary. Coordination, in spite of the difficulties, is essential in order to not only assure the needed levels of services and facilities in all populated parts of regions, but also to minimize duplication and waste of funds and personnel. Medical facilities planning is increasingly recognized as a major responsibility of metropolitan and regional planning agencies and is a geographic task.

Schools and Land Use

The public school system is a large user of urban land, a large employer, and a large consumer of local budgets. Precise measurements are difficult but, perhaps half the local tax revenue is spent to support public schools in the United States. The public school system obviously also depends heavily on urban streets and roads and even on pathways and sidewalks.

School location analysis is a geographic task but location is usually selected from inside the school system though often with the cooperation of the local planning department.

Recent forced racial integration of schools, in the United States including forced busing of students, has been in response to inequitable facility distribution and was surely long overdue from that standpoint. However, the long-range intent of forced integration is surely acculturation of the minority sub-culture. It remains to be seen whether or not forced school integration will be successful in this intent or, for that matter, whether acculturation is even desirable.

In many cities, private schools play an important role. Many people believe that the perceived deteriorating quality of public schools justifies the provision of alternative school systems. In some instances, private schools are devices for avoiding racial integration; in other instances they are desired by some people because of desire to combine religious with secular education, or to avoid certain aspects of public education which they believe to be in conflict with their religious beliefs. Some religious denominations, such as the Roman Catholic and Lutheran, maintain large city school systems. Some private schools, on the other hand, are secular and non-denominational. In any event, non-proprietary private schools are tax-exempt, whether maintained by a religious organization or not, on the grounds that if they did not exist the public would have to pay for larger school systems than at present.

Nearly all public school systems and many private school systems are hierarchically organized. Spatially, they commonly conform to the "central place" model. Local neighborhood elementary schools feed into community high schools, whose service area embraces that of several elementary schools. In some instances there is an intermediate level: that of the "middle school" or "junior high school", with a service area intermediate between that of the elementary school and the high school. Community colleges, which have been proliferating for several decades, serve still larger areas, and draw from several or many high schools. Four-year colleges and universities, in turn, whether primarily regionally- or nationally-oriented, are fed from still more extensive areas.

Religious Land Uses

Neighborhoods and communities have widely diverse requirements for religious institutional sites, and it is sometimes difficult for a developer, especially in the suburban fringe areas, to anticipate the needs. Commonly, in large-scale developments, sites may be set aside for churches, but the religious complexion of the future residents may be unknown.

Most sites for religious institutions create a demand for parking areas which are more extensive than the sites of the buildings themselves. Although typically the zoning ordinances permit churches and synagogues in residentially-zoned areas, the parking requirements may exercise constraints upon the location of the institutions.

Where the population of a community or neighborhood is mainly of one religious denomination, a single church site may serve the demand. On the other hand, heterogeneous residential areas may involve need for several, or many, churches and/or synagogues. Ethnic neighborhoods may be associated with certain denominations, and the ethnicity may be the major determinant of the number and location of the churches. Inner city areas may have ethnic parishes of some denominations, such as Roman Catholic and Eastern Orthodox. On the other hand, some churches may attract city-wide or even metropolitan-wide congregants: in such event the parking requirements may be much greater than for the more localized institutions. Orthodox Jews who are observant do not ride to and from services on the Sabbath: consequently they form concentrated ethnic communities, commonly with several or many small synagogues within a relatively small area. On the other hand reform and some conservative Jewish congregations serve very extensive areas and may attract participation from an entire metropolitan area. Some denominations, such as the Roman Catholic, tend to a hierarchical organizational structure; in such instances certain churches - or cathedrals - may be much more important, and may be located on more prominent or conspicuous sites than others.

In general, structures (and land which they occupy) used for religious purposes are tax-exempt. In some municipalities where there are very extensive areas used by religious organizations, the fiscal problems of the local governments may be intensified by the need to service such institutions and areas while receiving little if any revenue from them. Some alternative payments in lieu of taxes may mitigate the problems to a limited extent.

Public Safety

Fire Protection — The fire departments of the cities of the world function for the prevention and control of undesirable fires. Instant communication and computer information systems have freed firemen and equipment from stationary locations and permitted more emphasis on inspection and thus on the prevention function. Nevertheless, a fire out of control is a freightening and dangerous situation, so fire control is still the more visible part of the fire department function.

The spatial pattern of fire stations in the United States is dictated by an association of fire insurance underwriters. Specifications require certain hydrant fire flows and certain fire station distances for various land use categories. The municipality must submit a plan and map locating different categories of present and proposed fire stations in accordance with insurance guidelines. If the plan is under implementation on a reasonable time schedule the city is awarded a favorable insurance rate schedule. If implementation falters, or if no plan is submitted, insurance rates become less favorable.

Fire station categorization and location is a geographic task. For many years the task was assigned to city planning departments. Recently, however, the fire departments of medium sized and large cities have appointed people of their own to work as applied geographers.

City fire departments are users of land for fire stations. Fire departments are important users of the street and road network. Fire departments also depend on accurate locational references in order to get to an out-of-control blaze in as short a time as possible.

Police Protection — Police departments function for the maintenance of law and order through enforcement of criminal codes and/or the prevention of criminal acts and/or the apprehension of persons suspected of criminal acts. In actuality, the police chief and his department also often enforce the moral standards of the city, suburb, or exurb by the manner in which the law is enforced. This is possible because most jurisdictions contain a matrix of archaic, even foolish, laws along with the sound ones. These "bad" laws lend themselves to selective enforcement, usually to the detriment of the poor and to the minorities.

Citizens' groups have suggested that not only should archaic laws be stricken but, all laws involving "crimes without victims." Such victimless crimes would include intoxication, vagrancy, gambling, Sunday closings, prostitution, sex acts between consenting adults (including homosexuality), pornography, drug use, and disturbing the peace (except for specific infractions). If policing of morals and victimless crimes were to be eliminated, as many people advocate, policing of real crimes and the effectiveness of police organizations could be greatly increased. In terms of land use, there could possibly be a slight decrease in the number of police stations.

There are numerous ways in which the demand for police protection can be reduced with consequent increases in the effectiveness of the police. Landscaping of city parks can be redesigned to reduce the possibility of hiding places for prospective attackers of those who use the parks. Commercial districts can be made more attractive for evening and nighttime uses. Use of cash for business transactions can be reduced, thus reducing the potential for muggings and robberies, by greater dependence upon non-negotiable checks, credit cards, charge accounts, and computer transfer of funds.

In residential districts the neighborhood watch, or eyes on the street programs, have been effective in reducing crime. The components of these programs are good locks — kept locked, cash out of the house, and keep an eye on the neighborhood and on the houses. Anything suspicious should be reported to the police with no harm done if the person or action was innocent.

Police departments are users of land for police stations, and users of street and road network. Police depend on accurate locational references in order to get to a crime scene quickly. Effective police departments, however, must predict where and when crime will occur. This is accomplished by plotting, crime locations by time and season then analyzing these data. This is a geographic task but the applied geography is almost always performed from inside the department. In recent years some academic geographers have conducted studies of the spatial aspects of urban crime. They commonly relate the crime statistics on homicides, rapes, burglaries, robberies, and other aspects of social morbidity to the socio-economic differences between and among the communities within cities.

Solid Waste Collection and Disposal

Solid waste disposal is primarily an urban problem (although agricultural waste can also be a significant problem) and is the leading cause of urban land pollution.

Solid waste can be burned, compacted, shredded, subjected to pyrolysis (high temperature, low oxygen burning), composted, buried, or simply dumped. No matter; it ends on or under the ground and pollutes the land, the water, and the air.

The problems connected with solid waste are: (1) collection (2) transportation and (3) disposal. Of the three, transportation is the costliest although all three problems are closely intertwined.

Solid waste disposal is a formidible problem. Two of the more esoteric suggestions have been to hurl solid waste into space or hydrogen bomb it. In both cases transportation to the site and disposal would be prohibitively costly. Burying is the only practical solid waste disposal method yet devised.

Sanitary landfill is the best known method for burying solid waste. The material is dumped in a hole in the ground and covered with soil daily. Landfill is about the same except covering is done only periodically. Open dumping, however, is still the most prevalent disposal method in the world and in the United States. Open dumping creates unpleasant odors, draws rats, and is a potential disease causer. It must cease.

Problems associated with landfilling are: 1) generation of methane gas, which is toxic and explosive and moves through the earth, 2) Settling, which precludes building on the landfill site for many years, and 3) ground water pollution.

The greatest problem associated with landfilling, however, is behavioral. No one wants a "garbage dump" near his residence and he'll "vote the rascal out" who suggests it. The behavioral aspect has almost completely negated rail haul to abandoned mines in adjacent states. One state will not accept another's garbage.

Pyrolysis is becoming increasingly popular, especially in large cities, where nearby landfill sites are scarce. Although pyrolysis is quite expensive and requires the burying of residue, its relative cost is not prohibitive when long hauls to distant landfill sites are the alternatives.

There is no definitive answer to the problem of solid waste disposal. It is only possible to reduce its magnitude through recycling, shredding, and compacting.

Recycling of solid waste is a collection problem. To be economically feasible, solid waste recycling must take place before everything is mixed together. The retrieval of useable materials after collection and haul is difficult and costly.

A recycling program requires study. The make-up of solid waste must be determined as well as the demand for each constituent. The solid waste producer, whether home or factory, must be persuaded to separate the constituents. This can probably be accomplished through financial incentives. The constituents must be collected separately and moved to a transfer station (shredded, compacted, bailed, etc.) and the remainder is shredded and compacted for transportation to the landfill. If pyrolysis is to take place it is done at or near the landfill. Although the reusable materials are sold, the primary advantages to the program are 1) prolonging landfill life and 2) reducing costly hauls. This is no small matter inasmuch as transportation accounts for about 80 percent of the cost of the entire operation.

Water and Sewer Systems

From a spatial standpoint water and sewer systems are potent tools for guiding the direction or urban growth. Private wells and septic tanks, although sound in theory, do not always operate well in practice. The availability of water and sewer services is a powerful locational device for new subdivisions. The wise planner uses these tools to further the comprehensive areawide urban or metropolitan plan.

Sewage, whether residential or industrial, flows through large pipes, termed outfalls, to treatment plants downstream from the urban area. The location of the treatment plants relative to the urban area has great impact on urban growth and development. Pumping sewage uphill is a very expensive process; only those developments upstream of the treatment plant can count on tapping into the sewer system. Thus treatment plant location as well as outfall routes have considerable influence on the direction of urban growth.

Sewage treatment is a three stage process. Primary treatment consists of settling, and is considered about 25 per cent efficient. Secondary treatment adds aeration and bacterial action and is considered about 90 per cent efficient. Tertiary treatment adds filtration and is considered 99 per cent efficient. However, these treatments do not remove toxic chemicals or metals. Since some of the metal and chemical pollution is irreversible the problem needs study before the waters of the earth become hopelessly polluted.

At one time cities relied on single combined sewer systems for both sanitation and storm drainage. Storms or heavy rainfall tended to overload the combined systems and much of the effluent during these periods was dumped raw into the streams. Although there are many remaining combined systems, many cities now have dual systems.

While separate storm sewer systems function better than combined systems, there are still problems. Pesticides, herbicides, salt, detergents, sediment, dog feces, litter, petroleum products, metals, and chemicals are dropped in the street and flushed downstream during periods of rainfall. Sewage disposal is, as yet, not a completely solved problem.

Water lines usually serve the same places as sewer lines, and together they have a powerful influence on subdivision location. On occasion, water and not sewer is furnished and, even by itself, is more desirable than private wells and is thus a subdivision guidance system.

Water is becoming in short supply in many urbanized countries. Transportation over long distances or desalinization of sea water are both very expensive, so cities must depend on nearby surface or ground water. As supplies become critical during the next twenty years, it would seem that recycling is the only realistic answer. Recycling is technically feasible but poses a behavioral problem. People do not like the thought of reusing the water that once carried their own wastes. Considerable education is necessary before recycling will become widely adopted.

Until water recycling is feasible, conservation is a necessity. For example, less water will be used if pricing curbs are applied. Seepage could be eliminated from distribution systems. Alternative sources for different uses would require separate distribution systems but may become necessary before complete recycling is a reality.

Parks and Recreation

City park locations commonly conform to **The Central Place Theory.** Urban parks are seen as a four part hierarchy consisting of playlots, neighborhood, community, and regional parks. Since each higher order performs all the functions of lower orders plus a set of functions that sets them above the lower orders, urban parks neatly fit the central place hierarchy.

Playlots should theoretically be scattered throughout the residential sections of the urban area; a short walk for all residents. Benches and play equipment (slides, swings, etc.) are furnished and ''lot-size'' space is all that is necessary. Neighborhood parks are up to ten acres in size. They contain the equipment of the playlot plus grass, trees, walks, and enough space to throw a frisbee or a softball. A neighborhood park functions as a playlot for those who live within a block or two. Nevertheless, a neighborhood park should be within walking distance (½ mile) of all residents. Community Parks function as neighborhood parks and/or playlots for those who live close enough, but in addition they contain athletic fields, swimming pools and the like. Community parks are up to fifty acres in size and should theoretically be no more than five miles from any resident. Regional parks perform all the functions of the lower orders plus picnicing, hiking, boating, zoos, nature trails, nature or botanical displays, and sometimes golfing. Regional parks typically are in excess of one hundred acres in size and should be no more than ten miles from all residents.

Private parks are not arranged hierarchically but serve the outdoor recreation needs of higher income areas. Usual functions are tennis and swimming. The value of private parks to the city or local government is one of substitution. Where private parks exist the local government need not furnish public parks and the money can be spent in lower income areas.

Country Clubs are private parks. They usually include tennis courts and swimming pools, as well as golf courses. They serve higher income areas in lieu of public parks but perform the added function of raising nearby residential land values. Residential land values are higher than normal for the location, in a so called country club district.

Urban parks, whether public or private, are primarily for use. Nevertheless, they can also serve the person who has never touched a frisbee or munched a hot dog in the open air. To some, parks are an esthetic delight, to others a part of their heritage. Parks can also be appreciated from afar.

Recreation preserves, at a distance from the central city serve the central city and the surrounding area. They add to the urban area's economic base by making the sale of recreational accouterments (boats, motors, skis, fishing equipment, etc.) feasible. They preserve open space, they preserve wild life for further recreational purposes, and they can help avoid pollution in water sheds serving the urban area.

Use of recreation preserves falls off dramatically beyond an hour's driving time. Since these preserves are important to the urban area their location should be carefully planned.

Private owned vacations homes have an effect on an urban area. Although most vacation homes are within an hour or two of an urban area, nevertheless, during the periods of occupancy they reduce the need for urban services and utilities and drain money (spent elsewhere) from the economic base.

Urban Density and Public Services

For each level of public service, there is a "threshold", or minimum level of supporting population. This varies depending upon the financial requirements of the service and the income level of the population in the supporting areas but seems to be about 2000 persons per square mile, although these are wide variations. Where population densities are high, the services need to be more intense, and the facilities spaced more closely. Where the population density is less, the costs of overcoming the friction of distance are greater, and either the level of service which can be provided is lower, or the facilities are spaced farther apart, or both. In order to provide the same level of services in lower density areas as in higher density areas, a community, if it does not wish to subsidize the low-density areas, which tend commonly to be more affluent than the high-density ones, must charge more for the services. It is, therefore, quite realistic for suburban transportation to cost more per passenger-mile than that in the inner city, and for sewer, water, and other delivery services to have a higher level of charges, although this is not always the case. In fact, it is not unusual for middle density (middle income) areas to partially subsidize both the low density (affluent) and the high density (low income) areas through service charges and property taxes. The affluent do not always pay the full cost of services and the poor do not always pay adequate taxes.

SELECTED READINGS

Baumann, Duane E., and Daniel Dworkin, *Water Resources for Our Cities*. Resource Papers for College Geography No. 78-2. Washington: Association of American Geographers, (1978), 35 pp.

Cain, Louis P., *Sanitation Strategy for a Lakefront Metropolis: The Case of Chicago*. De Kalb: Northern Illinois University Press, (1979), 161 pp.

Christianson, Jon B., "Evaluating Locations for Outpatient Medical Care Facilities", *Land Economics*, Vol. 52, No. 3 (August, 1976), pp. 299-313.

Claire, William H., "The Church in the City Plan", *Journal of the American Institute of Planners*, Vol. 20, No. 4 (Fall, 1954), pp. 174-177.

Clayton, Kenneth C. and John M. Huie, *Solid Wastes Management: A Regional Solution*. Cambridge, Mass.: Ballinger Publ. Co., (1973), 135 pp.

Dear, Michael, "Locational Factors in the Demand for Mental Health Care", *Economic Geography*, Vol. 53, No. 3 (July, 1977), pp. 223-240.

Earickson, Robert, *The Spatial Behavior of Hospital Patients: A Behavioral Approach to Spatial Interaction in Metropolitan Chicago*. University of Chicago Department of Geography Research Paper No. 124, (1970), 138 pp.

Goetsch, Herbert A., "Community Facilities Planning:, in: Wm. H. Claire (editor), *Handbook on Urban Planning*. New York: Van Nostrand Reinhold Company, (1973), pp. 175-194.

Gold, Seymour M., "Recreation Space, Services and Facilities", Chap. 10 of: *The Practice of Local Government Planning*. Washington: International City Management Association, (1979), pp. 273-299.

Greenberg, Michael R. *et. al.*, "A Geographical Systems Analysis of the Water Supply Networks of the New York Metropolitan Region", *The Geographical Review*, Vol. 61, No. 3, (July, 1971), pp. 339-354.

Griggs, Gary B. and Gilchrist, John A., "Waste Disposal and Treatment", Chap. 9 of: *The Earth and Land Use Planning*. North Scituate, Mass.: Duxbury Press, (1977), pp. 327-365.

Hall, Sam L., and Rogers, Michael P., "Reexamining the Federal Role in Meeting Urban Recreation and Open Space Needs", *Urban Land,* Vol. 37, No. 11 (December, 1978), pp. 7-13.

Hackscher, August, *Open Spaces: The Life of American Cities.* New York: Harper & Row, (1977), 386 pp.

Kelnhofer, Guy, Jr., *Metropolitan Planning and River Basin Planning.* Atlanta: Georgia Institute of Technology, Water Resources Center, 1968, 208 pp.

Kloetzli, Walter, and Arthur Hillman, *Urban Church Planning.* Philadelphia: Muhlenberg Press, (1958), 186 pp.

Laurie, Ian C. (editor), *Nature in Cities: The Natural Environment in the Design and Development of Urban Green Space.* New York: John Wiley & Sons, (1978), 428 pp.

Leopold, Luna B., *Hydrology for Urban Land Planning: A Guidebook on the Hydraulic Effects of Urban Land Use.* Circular 554, U.S. Geological Survey. Washington: U.S. Government Printing Office, (1972).

Maxfield, Donald W., "Spatial Planning of School Districts", *Annals of the Association of American Geographers,* Vol. 62, No. 4 (December, 1972), pp. 582-590.

Mayer, Jonathan D., "Response Time and its Significance in Medical Emergencies", *The Geological Review,* Vol. 70, No. 1 (January, 1980), pp. 79-87.

Morrill, Richard E., et. al., "Factors Influencing Distances Traveled to Hospitals", *Economic Geography,* Vol. 46, No. 2 (April, 1970), pp. 161-171.

Norton, Perry L., *Church and Metropolis.* New York: Seabury Press, (1964), 128 pp.

Parsons, Kermit C. and Davis, Georgia K., "Education Services", Chap. 11 of: *The Practice of Local Government Planning.* Washington: International City Management Association, (1979), pp. 300-329.

Platt, Rutherford H., *The Open Space Decision Process: Spatial Allocation of of Costs and Benefits.* University of Chicago Department of Geography Research Paper No. 142. (1972), 189 pp.

Pyle, Gerald F., *Heart Disease, Cancer and Stroke in Chicago: A Geographical Analysis with Facilities Plans for 1980.* University of Chicago Department of Geography Research Paper No. 134, (1971), 292 pp.

Shannon, Gary W. and Dever, G. R. Alan, *Health Care Delivery: Spatial Perspectives.* New York: McGraw-Hill, (1974).

Skitt, J., *Disposal of Refuse and Other Waste.* New York: Halsted Press, John Wiley & Sons, (1973), 405 pp.

U.S. Executive Office of the President, Office of Science and Technology, *Solid Waste Management: A Comprehensive Assessment of Solid Waste Problems, Practices and Needs.* Washington: U.S. Government Printing Office, (May 1969), 111 pp.

Van Burkalow, Anastasia, "The Geography of New York City's Water Supply: A Study of Interactions", *Geographical Review,* Vol. 49, No. 3 (July, 1959), pp. 369-386.

CHAPTER NINE

Land Used For Transportation

Transportation and land use are two sides of the same coin. Most cities exist primarily for exchange of goods and services with the rest of the world, for which transportation is obviously essential. At the same time internal movement of people and goods binds together the mutually complementary and specialized land uses within cities.

Land devoted to transportation in most cities and metropolitan areas of the United States and Canada constitutes from one-fourth to half or more of the total developed area. This includes highways, streets and alleys as well as off-street parking areas devoted to the motor vehicle in motion and at rest, and the rights-of-way and terminal facilities or inter-city and inter-regional carriers: railroads, trucks, ships, barges, aircraft, and pipelines.

There is no inherent demand for transportation as such. The demand arises from the need to give goods and people what economists call "place utility": to place them where they are useful and productive, or, in the case of people, where their demands for goods and services can be satisfied. Without transportation, each place must be self-sufficient. In some respects transportation and communication are competitive. With rapid development of electronic communication, including two-way cable television and terminals connected to computer networks, it is possible that per capita demand for transportation, especially passenger transportation, may greatly decrease in the future.

About twenty percent of the gross national product of the United States is devoted to transportation, and about one of every five workers is involved in performance of transportation. The automobile, of course, is almost ubiquitous, and most Americans are almost totally dependent upon it for their personal movement, while trucks move more than sixty percent of the merchandise and one-quarter of all goods in domestic trade. There are as many miles of highway and street as there are square miles of land in the coterminous United States.

Transportation Costs and Land Costs

Ideally, the least cost of overcoming the friction — and thus cost — of distance would be to minimize demand for transportation, by developing interacting land uses as near each other as possible. But two objects cannot occupy the same space at the same time, and in many cities there are areas of extreme congestion because each establishment seeks to occupy land as close as possible to the others with which it interacts. The result is competition for the most accessible land. This drives up the costs ("site rentals") of the land in high-density areas. Each prospective land user must balance the high land costs of centrality against the higher costs of transportation and communication which result from locating farther away, and hence in areas of lower density. This results in a negative exponential "distance decay" relationship which is discussed elsewhere in accordance with an analog of the law of gravitation.

Transportation systems require vehicles, motive power (energy), and land, as well as organizations to perform the service. Transportational land is devoted to rights-of-way (routes, between origins and destinations) and terminals for the assembly and distribution of freight and passengers, as well as facilities for the storage and servicing of the vehicles, roads, railroads and other physical plant.

Planners and geographers are concerned with several separate but inter-related aspects of transportation in urban areas:

1. **Traffic,** which is the total of all individual movements, during a given period of time, between an origin or region of origins and a destination or region of destinations;

2. **Routes,** which are the paths between origins and destinations. Routes are rarely straight lines (or, for great distances, great circles) which are the shortest distances, but are usually more-or-less circuitous, either because of terrain conditions, the configurations of land and water, climatic conditions, or the desire to tap intermediate sources of traffic between origins and destinations. Routes converge at *nodes,* forming *networks.* At the nodes, routes (links, sectors) *interface:* traffic is interchanged (transferred) between links, and between carriers of the same or different nodes. When the interchange is between different modes, as, for example, between truck and rail, or between rail and ship, the movement is said to be *intermodal.* In any event, the collection and loading of people and goods, their unloading (discharge) and distribu-

TRANSPORTATION COSTS

Fig. 9

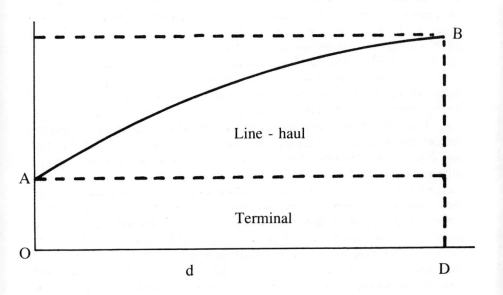

In the figure above, OA represents the terminal costs at both ends of a movement; d represents the distance between the origin O and destination D over distance d. BD is the total marginal cost of transportation between origin and destination OD.

tion, and their transfer between and among carriers, requires extensive facilities, which, in many instances, occupy large tracts of land; these are:

3. **Terminals,** including railroad freight yards, passenger depots and accessory facilities truck and bus terminals, port terminals, airports, and "tank farms" associated with pipelines. Automobile parking areas, including areas used for curbside parking on the streets, offstreet garages and parking lots, as well as the areas on residential land used for parking of automobiles, may also be regarded as terminals. With the growth of inter-city trucking for merchandise movement, and TOFC (trailer-on-flatcar: railroad "piggybacking"), the loading docks at commercial and industrial establishments have increased in importance as terminals.

Costs of movement between terminals are called *line-haul* costs, and they vary with distance. Terminal costs, on the other hand, are largely fixed, and are independent, for the most part, of the distance of the movements. In Figure the horizontal axis represents distance (d), and the vertical axis represents the cost of movement. For some transportation, the cost of movement is independent of distance, as, for example, the cost of moving a letter between origins and destinations anywhere in the nation. Some movements cost the same per mile regardless of distance. Still others cost less for each successive distance unit, such as a mile, than for the preceeding unit; in such instances, which are most common in inter-city and inter-regional transportation, the cost curve flattens with increasing distance. Such a curve is a "distance taper". If the distance is short, terminal costs represent a higher proportion of the total cost of the movement than for a longer-distance movement. For a given journey or shipment, the cost of transportation — the difference between cost at origin and cost at destination — is the sum of the fixed or overhead costs, such as depreciation, debt service, maintenance costs, and management costs of the carrier organization; the terminal costs, and the line-haul costs. In addition, there may be, and commonly are, certain "externality" costs, such as negative environmental impacts of transportation, which may or may not be quantifiable, and which usually do not represent direct costs to the shipper or traveler.

Transportation Modes

Each transportation mode is inherently best suited to carry certain types of traffic under certain conditions. The traveler or shipper determines the mode or combination of modes which produces, for the given trip or shipment, the optimum combination of time, cost, reliability and safety. The proportion of the total traffic which results is called the "modal split". Many public policy issues, such as the respective roles of automobile and public mass transportation of people within cities, are basically issues of modal split.

The relative roles of the various modes of transportation change over time. In intercity travel, for example, the railroad was the overwhelmingly dominant mode for many decades, but the automobile is now predominant; it was responsible for about eighty-five percent of all inter-city passenger miles of travel in the United States, while all other modes compete for the remainder. The automobile is also dominant in local circulation, except in portions of a few of the largest cities and metropolitan areas, where high density makes automobile usage difficult and unduly costly to the public, while at the same time the high density makes use of mass transit both feasible and imperative. In the late nineteenth and early twentieth century the trolley car was the major form of internal personal movement within most American cities. After decades of automobile dominance, with the principal, but less important, mass transportation mainly by uses, rail transit is making a revival in some metropolitan areas. In freight transportation the railroads still produce more ton-miles than any other mode, but the "commodity mix" is such that the railroad freight tonnage consists mainly of bulk commodities such as coal, ores, and grain, whereas the over-the-road intercity trucks carry much higher proportions of the merchandise and manufactured goods traffic.

The proportion of domestic intercity and inter-regional movement of goods and people in the United States during a recent year is shown in Table 3.

TABLE 3

PERCENTAGE DISTRIBUTION OF INTERCITY DOMESTIC FREIGHT AND PASSENGER MOVEMENT IN THE UNITED STATES
1980

Mode	Percent of freight ton-miles	Percent of passenger - miles
Railroads	37.10	0.75
Highways	22.70	85.06a
Inland Waterways b	16.90	-
Oil pipelines	23.10	-
Domestic airways c	0.20	14.19
Total	100.00	100.00

a. Includes: automobiles 83.28 percent, and buses, 1.77 percent.
b. Includes Great Lakes.
c. Includes airlines and private plane operations.

SOURCE: U.S. *Bureau of the Census Statistical Abstract of United States 1980*. Washington: U.S. Government Printing Office, 1981 and Motor Vehicle Manufacturers Association of the United States, Inc. *MVMA Motor Vehicle Facts and Figures*, Detroit, 1981.

For any given shipment or trip, some modes have lower line-haul costs than others, while some have lower terminal costs but higher line-haul costs. *Intermodalism* involves transfer of shipments or passengers between modes at intermediate points between origin and destination; these points are sometimes called *interfaces*. The costs and time consumed at interfaces as well as at origin and destination terminals are greatly reduced by *unitization*. Unitization involves putting the ladings into standardized containers and substituting capital-intensive equipment, such as specialized cranes and other materials-handling equipment, for individual handling of each piece. Individual handling is much more labor-intensive. Thus, mechanization of cargo transfer for package freight (general cargo) has produced economies of scale, somewhat analogous to those earlier achieved by mechanization of continuous-flow bulk commodities.

Land-Use Impacts of Unitized Cargo Handling

There are several methods of unitized general cargo handling, the adoption of which has been very rapid in recent years.

One method is *containerization,* which has greatly facilitated intermodal transfer. Containers are standardized metal boxes, designed for movement by ship, rail or truck, transferred by special equipment such as cranes, which commonly are located on the wharves or at "ramps" where truck-rail transfer is accomplished expeditiously. The containers aboard ship are stacked on deck and in cellular holds, and may be transferred between ship and shore either by shoreside cranes, some of which are specially designed for the purpose, or by lifting devices aboard ship. On some major transoceanic routes, over eighty percent of the general cargo traffic is now containerized, in spite of the fact that the technique, for the most part, was developed only within the past quarter century. In North America, containerization has facilitated the development of the "land bridge" and "mini bridge", whereby railroads, and to a lesser degree highway carriers, transport overland the containerized shipments to and from ocean ports. The "land bridge" movements involve transcontinental movements of cargo between coasts - Atlantic, Pacific, Gulf of Mexico, and Great Lakes - of traffic having a water crossing at both ends, as, for example, between Japan and Europe, in competition with the Panama Canal, Suez Canal, round-Africa and Trans-Siberian routes. "Mini bridge" refers to traffic with a water link at one end only, but with overland movement to or from a port other than the nearest one equipped to handle it. Scale economies produced by such unitized cargo handling, together with the very large investments required in port-associated land and in equipment at the waterfront, is producing a concentration of traffic at fewer but larger and much more efficient ports ("load centers"). Many ports must face the problem of declining traffic, and need to plan for the re-use of port-associated land no longer needed for port purposes.

Another rapidly growing method of handling intermodal merchandise traffic is called RoRo ("Roll on Roll Off") in which freight, whether in semi-trailers, standardized containers on flatbed trucks, is moved on or off ships across ramps, without being removed from the wheeled vehicle, which is then transported by ship to another port, where the reverse transfer takes place.

Ocean-going container ships and RoRo vessels tend to be much larger than the typical "break bulk" general cargo vessels. They represent much larger capital investments per ship, and therefore can less afford time spent in ports in the loading and discharge of cargo. Whereas a medium-sized general cargo ship typically may spend from ten days to two weeks or longer in port, a much larger container or RoRo ship can frequently "turn around" in one day, or even in a single working shift, with use of a small fraction of the longshore labor force that was formerly required.

On the other hand, faster turn around of modern container and RoRo ships means that much more cargo can be transferred in less time. The movement between land and water carriers cannot be perfectly synchronized in time: cargo must be assembled awaiting ships, and must be stored in transit awaiting overland movement; this requires much larger tracts of land ajacent to waterfronts than was formerly required for breakbulk cargoes. The piers and slips familiar in the older sections of many ports, such as Boston, New York, Philadelphia, Baltimore, San Francisco and Seattle, are now obsolete, not only because of their design, but also because of limited landward access and confined areas for staging of cargoes, resulting in landward congestion and intolerable delays. Most older ports had their principal general cargo terminals located in proximity to the central cores of the cities, where other congestion augmented the problems of landward access to and from the port terminals. The ever-larger ships not only required deeper access channels, but also, because they could carry greater loads, more land area for staging. Such land is not generally available in or near the central areas of the port cities. Therefore, port terminals, more and more, tend to be located farther from the city cores, where more land can be made available for port terminal purposes at lower costs. At the same time, the need for deeper channels, and for faster and safer access of the deep-draft ships to and from the terminals, dictated a move seaward of many of the port installations. Thus the need for tug hire, pilotage, and other costs associated with the long, slow, and often hazardous passages through restricted channels between open water and the terminals is minimized, at the same time that the newer locations of port terminals in lower-density areas facilitates the provision of adequate highway access and railroad yards convenient to the waterfront marine terminals. This association of peripherally-located port terminals and associated landward facilities has also, in some instances, stimulated extensive manufacturing and warehousing activities, in which single-story structures can be provided on lower-cost and more adequately located land than their earlier multiple-story counterparts in the central areas of the cities. The Port of Oakland, California, for example, has acted as a large-scale developer of industrial parks. In an increasing number of port districts, foreign-trade zones have been established, commonly in locations convenient to the marine terminals. In such zones, distributors and manufacturers can receive goods from abroad or from domestic sources, store the merchandise, or manufacture, convert, or package the inputs, free from payment of duty on the good unless or until they pass through a gate and enter the host country. In many instances, such foreign trade zones attract industries which re-export goods received from foreign countries to the same or other foreign countries free from any customs duties to the host country. Although such foreigh trade zones, or "free ports" have long been common outside the United States, there has, in recent years, been a proliferation of such zones in the U.S. Most are in proximity to maritime port terminal areas, some are associated with international airports, and a few are located elsewhere in the metropolitan areas, the goods being moved to and from them in bond.

Not all ports handling international shipments need have direct deep-water access. Shallow-draft barges, moved on inland waterways inaccessible to ocean-going ships, or to and from ocean ports with terminals having inadequate water depths alongside, can benefit from the development of "fishyback" or "kangaroo" ships, which carry freight in barges. The barges are lifted aboard ship by cranes mounted on deck, and placed aboard in a manner similar to containers. Such ships are called LASH ("lighter aboard ship") vessels. Other ships which carry barges lift them by means of stern elevators, on which the barges are floated, and then lifted; these are "Seabee" ships. Barge-carrying ships have, in some instances, reduced or eliminated dependence upon shore-based installations at the ports, since the barges can be moved far inland on the rivers and canals. LASH barges in international trade have been handled at such inland ports as St. Louis and Cincinnati, without break of bulk at the seaports. Abroad, such rivers as the Rhine and the Yangtse make ports hundreds of miles inland into potential international ocean ports with all-water movement.

Inter-city and inter-regional overland movement of freight is by inland waterway, railroad, and highway. Inland waterway ports resemble ocean ports in that the land requirements for port facilities and for port-associated industrial development are quite similar. On the other hand, the locational requirements for railroad and truck freight terminals are rather different, and have changed substantially with adoption of larger units and consequent economies of scale. The amount of urban land needed for terminals and for access routes to the terminals has changed, as well as have the locations.

Railroad Land Uses

Among the largest railroad uses of urban land are classification yards, where freight trains are assembled and disassembled. Such yards commonly occupy areas as much as five miles long and half a mile wide. Freight trains are much longer than in the past, and consequently tracks in the "bowl" of the main yard must, ideally, be slightly longer than the longest train that the yard is expected to handle. In addition, there must be arrival yards for handling the inbound trains awaiting classification, and departure yards for outbound trains. Modern freight trains often exceed a mile in length; consequently a sequence of yards may be several miles long, and sixty or more tracks in width. Associated with major classification yards are other facilities, such as repair shops, facilities for accomodation of train crews, and, very often, breakbulk freight houses as well as "piggyback" ramps.

Obviously, such classification yards constitute major land uses in many cities and metropolitan areas. Some were established in the nineteenth and early twentieth centuries, when the railroad was the primary carrier (rather than the motor truck) of intercity merchandise freight, and when pickup and delivery of goods within the urban areas was by horse and wagon, or by the now superceded method of "trap" and "peddler" railroad car which was switched successively to each of the industries providing or receiving less-than-carload freight, and which had private switch tracks. Nearly all railroads long ago ceased handling less-than-carload freight, except as TOFC ("piggyback") or COFC (container on flatcar) movements. For shippers of less-than-truckload lots, carloading companies — freight consolidators — provide the railroads with truckload or carload unitized shipments, and their facilities constitute elements of the urban transportational landscape.

Because of the shift of many industrial and commercial shippers away from the central areas of the cities, because of lower cost of land at and beyond the urban periphery, and because of the actual or perceived adverse environmental effects of freight operations, classification yards have, through the years, tended to be relocated away from the centers of the cities. This has, in turn been accompanied by and has stimulated many other changes in the patterns of land use.

During the heyday of the railroad as the dominant carrier of not only bulk freight, as at present, but also of merchandise freight, some metropolitan areas, such as Chicago, St. Louis, Kansas City, Louisville and Indianapolis, were provided with "belt lines"; circumferential railroads, either independently operated or singly or jointly operated by the trunk lines intersecting and interchanging traffic among the radiating trunk lines. These belt lines were major developers of industrial districts with certain "externalities" in common. Thus the Central Manufacturing and Clearing Industrial districts in Chicago, the Central Manufacturing District in Los Angeles, and many others, were originally developed by belt-line railroads. These organized industrial districts furnish to the manufacturing and wholesaling establishments neutral access to all railroads with which the belt lines interchange. At the same time the railroads benefit not only from the revenue derived from sale or lease of the industrial land, but also from the traffic which the industries furnish.

In some of the larger metropolitan areas which are railroad *"gateways"* (nodes on the rail network where interchange among the railroads and between railroads and other nodes is important) the railroad-developed industrial concentrations of industry constitute major portions of the total land available for industry. At the same time they are major traffic generators for the regional and local highway networks, not only for trucks but also in movement of employees commuting to and from the plants located in such districts. The railroads, along with utility companies, are leading promoters of industrial location in the metropolitan areas which they serve.

Because newer and more efficient freight terminals and classification yards tend to be located in areas peripheral to the earlier urban development, and often well beyond, economies of scale indicate the advantage of concentrating the classification of cars for entire railroad systems at a limited number of locations, there is a "filtering down" of many older yards, which formerly were major classification yards, to switching yards for industries in the immediate vicinity. But because many industries in such older industrial areas also tend to relocate on and beyond the edges of the urbanized areas, many older yards are vacated, along with the branch railroad lines that connect or lead to them. The re-use of such redundant transportational land formerly devoted to railroad use is a significant challenge to city planners, as well as to the railroads themselves. In many instances, such lands are located adjacent to central waterfronts, because railroads originally — and to some extent still — seek waterfront locations, where they could interchange freight with ships and barges, as well as serve the commercial and industrial establishments that originally located near waterfronts. The problem of re-use and redevelopment of such excess railroad land is analogous, and complementary to, the problem of redevelopment of waterfront lands which were formerly devoted to port use but which are no longer needed for such purpose for the reasons indicated earlier.

In addition to developing organized industrial districts, railroads have been active in the development of large-scale commercial, residential and other uses of their urban lands, especially in and near the downtown areas. Early in the twentieth century, the Pennsylvania and the New York Central railroads in building and rebuilding, respectively, their passenger terminals in midtown Manhattan, developed adjacent concentrations of office buildings and hotels. Some were built on "air rights" above the railroad tracks, where increases in land values subsequently provided important non-transportational revenues to the railroads while at the same time the proximity of hotels and high-density office activity attracted passengers, both intercity and commuter, to the respective railroads. At present, the revenues from the high-value land, among the highest in the world, associated with Pennsylvania Station and Grand Central Terminal furnish the Penn Central Corporation — successor to the original railroads but no longer a railroad itself — its most important single source of income. Some of the most important buildings in New York are constructed on air rights directly over the terminals. Those include Madison Square Garden over Pennsylvania Station, and the Pan Am Building over Grand Central Terminal. Unfortunately, the development of air rights over Pennsylvania Station resulted in destruction of the monumental terminal building. Grand Central Terminal, although constantly threated with destruction, still remains. A somewhat comparable development in Chicago, Riverside Plaza, was built over the Union Station, involving demolition of one of the station's two buildings. In the same city, the former Illinois Central — now Illinois Central Gulf — railroad, is the developer of Illinois Center, an extensive high-density cluster of skyscraper office buildings and hotels over a major portion of its downtown properties.

Truck Terminals

Motor truck terminals, like marine and railroad terminals, have tended to locate more and more toward and beyond the edges of the cities, for much the same reasons. The movement, however, has been somewhat less conspicuous, because truck terminals tend to be smaller, and the access routes also serve other traffic.

In a sense, every commercial, industrial, residential and institutional establishment is a truck terminal, as well as an automobile terminal. Truckload shipments originate and terminate, for the most part, at the shippers' and consignees' loading docks, while less-than-truckload shipments, as well as TOFC and COFC, require specific terminals. The former are consolidated at the establishments of the freight forwarders, or at the warehouses of large retail and other merchandisers. Typical locations are on and beyond the city edges, although there are concentrations of truck terminals in the inner portions of many cities, especially in the wholesale and light manufacturing "frame" areas, where many shippers' and consignees' establishments still remain, in spite of the general tendency for outward relocation. Attractions of the urban periphery, as the motor truck became increasingly important *vis a vis* the railroad for merchandise traffic, resulted in partial or complete evacuation of many such areas surrounding central business districts. This locational characteristic has been reinforced by the fact that, in many cities, express highways ("superhighways", "freeways") radiate outward from inner distributor loop highways which completely or partially surround the central downtown areas, thereby furnishing rapid access and egress in all directions. At the same time they traverse areas in proximity to the urban cores, on land which is low in cost because of decreased demand by commerce and industry. The low cost made public purchase of rights-of-way for the inner loop expressways relatively easy, while the high proportion of vacant land and low acquisition cost facilitated uses such as parking lots and garages, as well as truck terminals. Thus, truck terminals may be found in both central and peripheral locations within the urban areas.

Pipelines

Pipeline terminals occupy substantial tracts of land in and near urban areas. Although transportation of water in aquaducts is important in many cities, they, along with reservoirs, are generally considered as public utilities rather than as transportation facilities. Petroleum pipelines, however, are treated as transportation lines, and in the United States there are several hundred thousand miles of pipelines, both intercity and local.

There are three major types of intercity pipelines, other than aquaducts. They are: (1) crude oil pipelines, (2) product pipelines, and (3) natural gas pipelines.

Crude oil and product pipelines lead to and from refineries. Oil refineries are among the most automated of all industrial establishments, employing, generally, about two persons per acre. They are also one of the most capital intensive industries. The pipelines themselves are generally underground, although in places they are evidenced by pumping and booster stations, which occupy relatively small land areas. Refineries, on the other hand, are always conspicuous features of the landscape, and their effects upon the environment, and upon nearby land uses, are significant. Nobody likes to live near an oil refinery, not only because of hazards, real or imagined, but also because of unsightliness air pollution and odors, although environmental regulations in recent years have to some extent mitigated the adverse environmental effects. Refineries, although contributing relatively little employment in proportion to the extensive land areas which they occupy, generate heavy traffic by rail, and especially by highway, as the tanker trucks distribute the products. Many refineries receive all or portions of their crude oil inputs by tanker ship or barge, and also distribute by vessel; in such instances waterfront locations are, of course, essential. Like other "heavy" industries, waterfront refineries and "tank farms" for storage of petroleum and products are commonly located near concentrations of other industries. Because of the need for large areas of land, the perceived adverse environmental impacts, and the relatively low volumes of personal travel that they generate, they are most usually situated on the outskirts of the cities, in areas where the density of development is very low. Commonly they are associated with petrochemical plants or other industries to which they are symbiotically related.

Power Lines and Unit Trains

An important mode of transportation over long distances is the high-voltage electric power line. Electric generation may be resource-oriented, where the plant is located over, or in proximity to, a coal mine or a source of natural gas, or may be market-oriented, in which case the fossil fuels must be transported to the plant. Market-oriented electric plants are usually located on urban waterfronts, if such locations are available. This is not only because the fuels are received by water but also because power generation requires large quantities of water for generator cooling.

Whether or not the plant has a waterfront location, if it is coal-fired the chances are great that it receives coal, in part at least, by means of *unit trains.* Unit trains are trains permanently assigned to a particular run, as between a coal mine or mines and an electric plant. The equipment may be furnished in whole or in part by the power company, or it may be railroad-owned. In any event, unit train costs are generally competitive with transportation by water. Costs are minimized because the trains do not require intermediate switching in the classification yards, because the amount of rolling stock is minimized by regular round-trip cycling without intermediate delays, because the trains are in almost continuous operation (reducing crew requirements) and because the loading and discharge of the coal is highly mechanized. Although unit trains are also used for transportation of other bulk commodities, ranging from grain to iron ores and even orange juice, about eighty percent of the hundreds of unit trains in the United States transport coal, mainly between mines and electric generating plants. Although the first unit train in the United States was placed in operation as recently as 1960, such trains are currently carrying a very high proportion of the traffic of the railroads. Their proliferation has increased the frequency of trains on some railroad lines to the extent that local street traffic is seriously interrupted by the transit grade crossings.

Railroad Grade Crossings

Grade Crossings generally constitute a serious problem in many cities. They are not only a hazard to pedestrian and vehicular traffic, but in some instances they necessitate duplication of emergency facilities, such as police and fire stations and hospitals, because of the interruptions to traffic on streets which cross the railroads. The rapid increase in railroad coal traffic has exacerbated the grade crossing problem along some routes. Generally, the municipalities or other units of government responsible for streets and highways share with the railroads the costs of grade crossing maintenance or elimination, but resources of both are limited, and progress has been very slow toward resolution of the grade crossing problem nationally. In some instances, streets can be closed where they cross the railroads. Abandonment of thousands of miles of railroad lines in the United States, encouraged by recent legislation, is resulting in elimination of many grade crossings, but these typically involve lightly-used railroad lines on which train movements were slow and infrequent. In some instances, downgrading or elimination of one or more railroad lines serving common points, and concentrating the traffic on fewer lines thereby increasing justification for elimination of grade crossings on the lines having more frequent trains, may be a partial solution to the problem.

Airports and Cities

Air transportation, except for the automobile, is the most important mode of intercity, interregional, and international passenger travel, and it is also important in the movement of valuable and time-sensitive cargo and mail. The main advantage of air transportation, of course, is speed, but much of that advantage is lost if ground access to and from the airports is inadequate, if the design of the airport and terminal is inefficient, or if the airport of its terminal capacity is too small. Location and design of airports is a major challenge, involving a vast complex of inter-related problems including ground access, airspace utilization and control, environmental impacts upon other land uses both near to and farther from the airport, the employment at the airport and in airport-related activities including movement of people and goods to and from the places of work, the provision for expeditious movement of the land traffic generated by employees, air passengers and visitors to the airport and its nearby establishments, the control of air pollution and noise in the vicinities of the airports, and the resolution of many conflicts between the requirements of the regular air carriers on the one hand and general aviation activities on the other. The problems are especially critical because of the vast areas of land required for the airports, as well as the land outside the airports where controls are needed to prevent obstructions in the airspace.

There are about 15,000 airports of all types in the United States, but only a few hundred are "air carrier" airports with regular scheduled airline service. Except for military airports, all the others are "general aviation" airports. General aviation embraces all aviation activities other than military and the regular scheduled airline services. The civil airports of the United States constitute a system, with mutually complementary types.

Air carrier airports are classified by the Federal Aviation Authority (FAA) into several types, depending upon size, but all of the carrier airports within a given metropolitan area (called a "community" by the FAA) constitute a "hub". There are four categories of hubs: large, medium, small, and "nonhubs", depending upon the volume of passenger enplanements per year on the scheduled airlines. "Large hubs" are metropolitan areas, each with one or more air carrier airports, which enplane at least one percent of the passengers of the scheduled airlines of the nation in a given year. There are usually about 26 such large hubs, although the number changes from time to time. Certain general aviation airports have been designated as "reliever" airports in and near the hub communities. Reliever airports are those which justify certain public funding on the basis that they carry on general aviation activities which otherwise would congest the carrier airports and cause untenable conflicts between the airline operations and general aviation. Within each metropolitan area, the general aviation airports, the reliever airports, and the air carrier airports, constituting the local system, should be considered, and planned for, as a single metropolitan system of airports, in relation to other aspects of metropolitan land use and transportation. Because of long-term increases in flying, air traffic control over and near hubs is especially critical. Separation of airports and approach corridors involves considerable complexity, as does the regulation of land uses to prevent encroachments upon the navigable airspace, especially the corridors in the airport vicinities.

Because most of the major metropolitan areas of the nation are already served by major airports, and because the land areas of airports and the costs of development are extremely high, it is quite unlikely that more than very few new major airports serving large hubs will be sited and developed in the future. Commercial aircraft of the future will undoubtedly be designed to operate to and from airports no larger than those now existing; they may very well be designed to operate with shorter takeoff and landing distances, in order to be able to use more airports and thus serve more communities than at present.

The emergence of the commercial air transport industry in the United States from more than four decades of federal regulation of routes, rates and services, is, in the early 1980s, rapidly changing the nation's airline picture. This, in turn, is reflected in changes in airport demand. Major airlines (the 12 largest domestic airlines were called "trunks" until 1981) have the largest aircraft and concentrate heavily on connecting the "large hubs" and the "medium hubs". Their aircraft each carry typically from 100 to 400 passengers in addition to cargo and mail. Only large, and a few medium, hub airports can generate sufficient traffic to justify use of such large aircraft with reasonably frequent schedules. Consequently, the major airlines have tended to end their services to many communities which could not produce economic "load factors" for the large planes. Other airlines, the "second level" or regional airlines, took up the service to many such communities, using somewhat smaller planes, although for longer distances some of their planes are of the same types as those used on the medium-length runs of the major carriers. Deregulation in the early 1980s enable some former "second level" or "regional" airlines to initiate longer routes, including, in some instances, transcontinental and international routes, thus obscuring some of the former distinctions between trunks and regionals. Many of the latter which have expanded their routes are now designated as "nationals". Most of the "second level" airlines began as feeders to the trunks, connecting with them at hubs. Many trunks also developed their own regional services, feeding their main routes with smaller planes converging at a limited number of hubs on their respective systems. With deregulation, many feeder routes operated by the trunk airlines were taken over by "nationals" and, to a greater extent, by the smaller regionals. Meanwhile, since World War II and especially during the 1970s and early 1980s, more than two hundred "third level" airlines were established. These, generally known as "commuter" airlines, typically connect smaller communities, which cannot justify service by the larger airlines with the hubs. Many commuter lines were established by "fixed base operators" whose original and primary business is general aviation, such as charter, instruction, crop dusting, and other activities. Some of the former commuter airlines have expanded, with larger planes and longer routes. Thus there is a "filtering up" or steadystate situation, in which, as airlines give up service to the smaller communities, the next level of airline may take it up. With the end of federal regulation, leaving the airlines free to operate routes and services wherever they find them practicable, continuation of service to smaller communities which generate a minimûm amount of air traffic was temporarily assured, until the late 1980s, by continuation of federal subsidies to "third level" airlines which provide such service.

All air carrier airports of the United States receiving service by the majors and nationals are publicly owned, while other airports, including some with commuter service, may be either publicly or privately owned and operated. Permanency is much less assured for privately-owned, because owners may be tempted, as the urban areas expand, to sell their properties or convert them to other urban-oriented uses which may yield substantially higher economic returns. The result, in some metropolitan areas, is an acute deficiency of general aviation airports, and, along with it, overcrowding of air carrier airports by general aviation activities which may conflict with the use of the airports by the scheduled air carriers. To reduce such effects, the FAA has designated some airports in and near hubs as reliever airports, giving them preferential treatment in availability of federal funds for airport improvements, such as runway extensions and instrument landing facilities.

The large air carrier airports, in many instances, are the largest single continuous pieces of land in unified ownership and devoted to a single purpose. The original Chicago Municipal (now Midway) Airport, when opened in the 1920s, occupied a quarter-section (160 acres) of land. In the late 1930s it was extended to a full square mile, and by 1958 it had become the busiest airport in the world, handling ten million passengers in that year. After World War II Chicago acquired a small airport northwest of the city which was ancillary to a wartime airframe manufacturing plant, and the field was subsequently expanded to a full ten square miles (6,400 acres) or ten times the area of the field which it supplemented. Eventually it became O'Hare International Airport, the world's busiest, handling, in a peak year, over fifty million departing and arriving passengers, and employing within its boundaries over thirty thousand people, in addition to many more thousands within a few minutes driving time from the field. Some of the newer airports, such as the Dallas-Fort Worth airport, the Charles de Gaulle Airport near Paris, and the Mirabel Airport north of Montreal, embrace as much as a hundred square miles, including clear or use-restricted approach zones.

It is obvious that such large airports cannot be located close to the centers of the urbanized areas, or even close to their margins, because of high land costs, difficulties of land assembly, and conflicts with nearby urban land uses. Thus, there must be a compromise, on the one hand, between the need for large airfields and extensive clear airspace zones and low-density land uses in the zones, and on the other hand the need for easy and rapid access between the cities and the airports. Because of deconcentration of commercial, industrial and residential developments in and around cities, a decreasing proportion of the air traffic originates and terminates in the central areas, but access to the urban cores, nevertheless, remains important. On the other hand, surface movement between the airport and the numerous locations within the metro-politan area where air passengers and cargo originate and terminate must also be provided. In some instances, circumferential as well as radial highways provide access. In spite of their nodal importance, airports by themselves rarely justify provision of express highways primarily for airport access. In a few areas, first Cleveland in 1968, later Washington, Chicago, and prospectively some other metropolitan areas, rail rapid transit connects the central city core and some intermediate areas with the airport terminal, though, in such instances also, the transit lines carry other substantial traffic besides that to and from the airport.

Whether planning for a new airport or expansion of an existing one, many factors must be considered. Cost of the land at alternate locations, of course, is important. Relation to other airports in the same metropolitan areas or region may involve a large number of interrelated considerations including: the roles of the given airport relative to the others which constitute the regional or metropolitan airport system, such as the respective roles of major hub or air carrier airports, reliever airports, and general aviation airports, the possible conflicts in use of the airspace, the relation to patterns of local and metropolitan land uses and the functional areas within which the demand is generated, and the environmental impacts, especially noise and air pollution.

While most people agree that airports are essential, few want them near their homes. Buffer zones within the airports and clear zones beyond the ends of the runways are indispensable. If development has taken place in the airport vicinity, the initial planning or the expansion of the airport become very difficult. The greatest hazards to people and structures on the ground, as well as to the aircraft and their occupants, occur in trapezoidal zones extending for several thousand yards beyond the ends of the runways.

These areas are also those in which the noise associated with aircraft activity is the greatest. Planners use the concept of the "noise envelope" to determine the relative amounts of noise expected at various locations in the vicinities of airports (Figure 10).

Noise levels are generally measured in terms of "perceived noise levels in decibels" (PNdb) which includes not only the actual levels of noise, but also the effects of various octave bands upon persons on the ground. A jet aircraft, for example, has a higher noise pitch than does a propeller-driven aircraft with piston engines, and thus, with a given decibel level, is considered somewhat more objectionable. Some general aviation airports, as the result of objections from their neighborhoods, prohibit jet aircraft altogether, in spite of the fact that some jets actually have lower PNdb levels than some piston-engine planes. Properly, noise performance standards should be invoked, rather than restrictions against specific types of aircraft. On the other hand, technological developments in aircraft and engine design are reducing the noise impacts, and certain types of older jet aircraft used extensively in commercial air transportation must, under federal regulations, be phased out or retrofitted with less noisy engines.

Atmospheric conditions, such as frequencies of wind directions and velocities, as well as fog, haze and smoke, are significant in the selection, continuation, or expansion of airports. In some regions, snow and icing conditions are important considerations. Fog, haze and smoke reduce visibility. In spite of rapid advances in visibility-restricted landing and takeoff techniques, reduced visibility restricts the capacities of airports, resulting in cancellations or diversion of flights.

Freedom from obstructions in the airspace within the approach zones, incuding those beyond the runways as well as aircraft-turning areas, must be assured. Ideally, the public should secure title to the airspace involved, either by purchasing the land underneath, or purchasing the air rights above the land, which may then be devoted to other, non-incompatible, uses. But such purchase is rarely possible because of limited availability of public funds. Alternatively, zoning for height restrictions should be imposed (Figure 11). Height restrictions will prevent encroachment; if an existing airport is threatened by existing encroachments retroactive clearance may be very difficult to achieve. Expansion of the airport may be impossible. Another difficulty with height restriction zoning is that commonly the affected or desired clear zones may transcend the boundaries of a given administrative unit, such as a village or city, and cooperative agreements among the various governmental units whose areas include the airspace may be difficult or impossible.

If an airport site includes an insufficient area of level land, or is adjacent to existing development in one or more directions, it is sometimes possible to provide a larger area by leveling and grading, or by landfill into adjacent water areas. Boston's Logan Airport, New York's LaGuardia and Kennedy, Newark Airport, Washington National, and San Francisco airports, among others, utilized fill in adjacent shallow waterways to expand their areas or to lengthen their runways. But water-adjacent sites also have disadvantages; among them are greater fog frequency and some difficulties in visual reference to the ground

AIRPORT NOISE ENVELOPE

Cleveland Hopkins Airport

Fig. 10

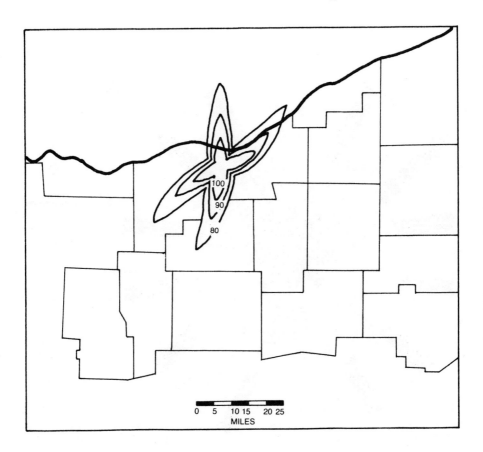

The airport noise envelope consists of a set of contours, measured in decibels of noise levels at various distances from the flight paths. In some instances the flight paths, especially on takeoff, are designed and constrained to minimize the noise and hazards on the ground, at the expense of somewhat reduced safety to aircraft and their occupants.

Source: *A Comparison of Regional Airport Sites in Northeast Ohio*. Kent State University Center for Urban Regionalism, April 1970.

145

RESTRICTION ZONES

CHICAGO O'HARE

Fig. 11

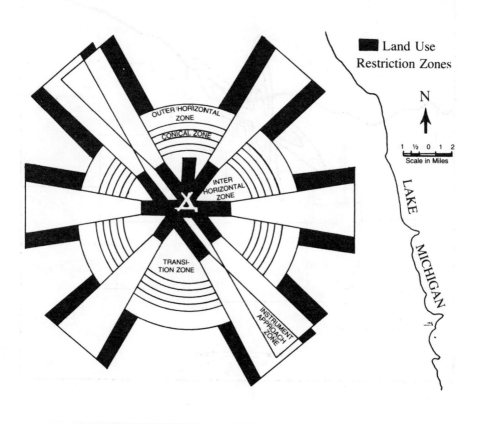

Restriction zones surrounding airports are a legal and viable zoning procedure.

Source: City of Chicago Department of Development and Planning

in landings, as well as lack of traffic-generating potential in the direction occupied by the water body where extensive bays are involved. Somewhat compensating is the absence of other development under the approach zones; water bodies are natural clear zones.

The intended functions of airports must be considered in determining their prospective size. Some large hubs have several air carrier airports, i.e. Kennedy and LaGuardia at New York, O'Hare and Midway in Chicago, Los Angeles International, Burbank, and Ontario as well as several others in southern California, Washington National, Dulles, and Baltimore-Washington International, etc. In some instances, the major or several major air carrier airports within or near the metropolitan area are supplemented by others closer to the city center, and commonly of smaller extent, which have supplemental air carrier service, usually with smaller planes; essentially commuter service. Some planes are of the STOL (Short takeoff and landing) type, enabling them to use much shorter runways. The rapid growth of commuter airlines in the late 1970s and early 1980s has renewed interest in airports close to the city centers. Some of them are predominantly general aviation facilities, and many were formerly the principal airports in the respective cities, as, for example, the Detroit City Airport, Dallas's Love Field, Houston's Hobby Airport, etc. Meigs Field in Chicago and Burke Lakefront Airport in Cleveland have scheduled services to cities up to a few hundred miles distance, in addition to considerable general aviation and commuter airline activity. Convenience to the central part of the city is the dominant consideration in continued operation of such airports.

Helicopters were, for a while, considered as prospective major connectors between centrally-located airports and the major air carrier airports more distant from the urban cores. Schedule helicopter services operated from downtown New York, Chicago and San Francisco, but were discontinued because of the complexities and high costs of maintenance of the aircraft, the public's adverse reactions after a series of accidents, and the high fares that were required. Small-scale scheduled helicopter operations were later resumed in several metropolitan areas. General aviation activity involving helicopter, however, is varied in urban areas, ranging from traffic surveillance and broadcasting of traffic reports to use of helicopter cranes for placing structural materials atop buildings, search and rescue activities, and emergency trips to hospitals. Downtown heliports exist in a few cities, as do rooftop landing pads, but some cities prohibit the latter.

In the larger metropolitan areas, airlines are reluctant to provide adequate numbers and frequencies of connecting services at, or between, major airports where more than one air carrier airport exists. Travelers will not generally favor transfer between flights at different airports, and the airlines cannot generally afford to maintain and operate duplicate facilities at more than one airport within a hub. Thus it is difficult to provide a "critical mass" of connecting flights at other than the principal airport within a given hub.

General aviation, in contrast to air carrier service, is carried on at thousands of airports; some metropolitan areas have numbers of them. With the rapid changes in scheduled airline service, and the smaller number of city pairs connected by frequent direct flights as larger planes have come into use by the majors and nationals, many commercial and industrial firms operate or charter planes for executive travel and time-sensitive shipments. Basing and servicing such business planes has become an important function of many general aviation airports. The location of such airports relative to each other, to the major airports, and to the general pattern of land uses and functional areas within the respective metropolitan regions, is critical. Many general aviation airports are in public ownership, but others are privately owned. Their retention and continued operation is constantly challenged as urban development expands and often surrounds them. Owners, whether public or private, are under frequent temptation to discontinue them and to sell off, or utilize themselves, the airport land for other uses which may yield a more direct economic return. On the other hand, such airports are important assets in industry and commercial activities which form major portions of a community's economic base, and in attracting new establishments.

Some general aviation airports may perform important functions as reliever airports, attracting general aviation which otherwise might contribute excessive congestion at the larger air carrier airports. In a number of instances, some scheduled services may also be available at reliever airports.

Internal Circulation

Cities and metropolitan areas could not function without means of moving people and goods from place to place within such areas. The division between internal movement on the one hand and external movement between the cities and metropolitan areas is not clear-cut. The express highways and major arterial streets carry both internal and external traffic, they furnish access to and from the railroad terminals, airports, port terminals and pipeline terminals, and they serve as rights-of-way for a variety of utilities. Some metropolitan areas have joint usage of railroad tracks by commuter trains as well as by intercity freight and passenter trains.

Street Systems

Street systems constitute the basic networks of internal circulation in virtually all cities. The oldest cities discovered by archeologists have street systems, not unlike those of today. Pompeii, after two millenia, reveals a system of streets, forming a rectangular grid, thus evidencing cental planning of the major elements of the city's spatial pattern, since all other land uses are related to street access. Today virtually all municipalities require street access as prerequisite to issuance of a building permit for any parcel of land, and street addresses are the principal means of orientation within cities.

Streets are multi-functional and, in a transportational sense, they are multi-modal. They accomodate pedestrians, animal-powered vehicles, private automobiles, taxicabs, police and fire vehicles and ambulances, trucks, street railway cars, buses, bicycles, motorcycles, and so forth. The rights-of-ways of streets also constitute, in some cities, the alignments of rapid transit rail lines, elevated and subway. In addition, they are the routes of utility lines: electric power lines, telephone lines, telegraph lines, cable television lines, gas pipelines, water distribution pipes, storm sewers, sanitary sewers, and, in some cities, steam lines and pneumatic tubes. Streets also constitute firebreaks, and in some places local streets may be cordoned off to function as temporary playgrounds. In some older portions of cities they serve a social centers, and, in effect, living rooms for socializing where the housing units lack such facilities. In many parts of the world, and more recently in the United States, lanes for bicycles have been designated in some streets. Finally, streets serve as the basic access to all developed parcels of land within the city: street addresses are essential. Some streets also serve as transportation terminals where offstreet parking is inadequate and the street widths permit.

Street systems are networks, each intersection constituting a node. Each street, between nodes, fits into a hierarchical arrangement, in which streets may be identified by their level in the hierarchy. These range from local access streets which are not intended, either by width, curvature or general alignment, to carry through traffic; collector streets; arterial or preferential streets; and limited access streets, which also may be "superhighways", "thruways", "expressways", or "freeways". Each of these successive levels of streets carries more traffic, with greater freedom from intersectional delays and medial and outer-lane frictions. Generally, each higher level has a lower accident rate in spite of higher traffic volumes.

Local access streets and collector streets have widths, if properly planned, in accordance with the density of traffic which they are intended to handle. In low-density residential areas, many such streets are too wide, with consequent inefficiencies since the land is not developed to the point at which maximum economic return is generated by the lesser number of housing units. Overly-wide streets may encourage undesirable through traffic in residential areas, and may also encourage use of the streets for parking whereas off-street parking should be used.

Arterial, or preferential, streets are intended to carry heavier volumes of traffic over longer distances, with less frequent — or preferably no — stops at intersections. Channelizing traffic, by means of dividers and "shadow lanes" at intersections to remove the vehicles awaiting their chance to make right or left turns, is common. Arranging traffic signals in sequence to permit through non-stop movement at relatively constant speeds is not uncommon, and such arrangements are facilitated where parallel streets carry one-way traffic, since such arrangement also reduces delays to cross-traffic. At some crossings of arterial streets, grade separations expedite traffic.

Many arterial streets and suburban arterial highways are lined by ribbons or strips of traffic-oriented business establishments, sometimes encouraged by obsolete zoning which provided for much more land than required for business use. During the heyday of the street railway, when cars could stop frequently, such ribbons tended to develop along their routes, and subsequently, local buses constituted a similar impetus for commercial ribbons along with the arterials. With the growth of outlying nucleated shopping and office centers, and with the decline of purchasing power in many older portions of cities, these ribbons declined, with high vacancy rates in the originally commercial buildings, and ultimately, physical decay and extensive demolition, leaving in their wake extensive areas of vacant land. With the ubiquity of the automobile and motor truck, many arterial streets have developed bottlenecks and safety hazards with numerous access and egress points associated with street-side establishments, and, frequently, with double-parking due to inadequate space at the curbs and lack of adequate offstreet parking.

Some routes within cities and metropolitan areas restrict traffic to certain types of movement or service, as, for example, prohibiting trucks. On the other hand, many urban communities designate certain streets as preferential for trucks, where the design and location as well as the types of pavements, are adequate.

Parkways and boulevards, use of which is generally confined to automobiles, with or without buses, constitute a special type of artery. The concept antedates the automobile, but in the 1920s and subsequently, when the automobile was still regarded primarily as a pleasure vehicle, numerous parkways were laid out in and near cities. A few have been re-built as modern expressways, but such up-grading is often resisted because it tends to change the character of the adjacent parkland.

Limited access streets and highways are those along which the abutting properties have no right of access. Access is provided at a limited number of places, where the design permits merging of traffic with minimal friction or delay. Many limited access routes are expressways or freeways, but some are conventional surface streets. Commonly, limited access routes are bordered by local access or frontage roads for local traffic, which may enter and leave the main arterial lanes at the controlled intervals.

The arteries with the highest capacities on which traffic moves at the highest speeds are the expressways or freeways. Streets and thoroughfares have considerable impact on both central city shape and metropolitan area pattern.

The basic shape of a central city, apparent from the air on a map, is one way to classify central cities. The value of such a classification system is its a priori aspect. It is one way the average person classifies cities. For example if you wished to describe the journey through Charleston, West Virginia to a friend making the trip for the first time, you might talk of the length of the city along the river (linear shape) along streets intersection at right angles (gridiron street pattern).

STREET PATTERNS

Fig. 12

Gridiron

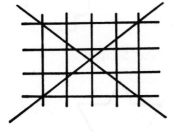

Radial/Circumferential

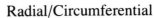

Gridiron/Superimposed Radials

Random

The diagram above represents four possible city street patterns. Although each occurs in many cities, there are also many cities that exhibit a combination of two or more of the patterns.

CENTRAL CITY SHAPE

Fig. 13

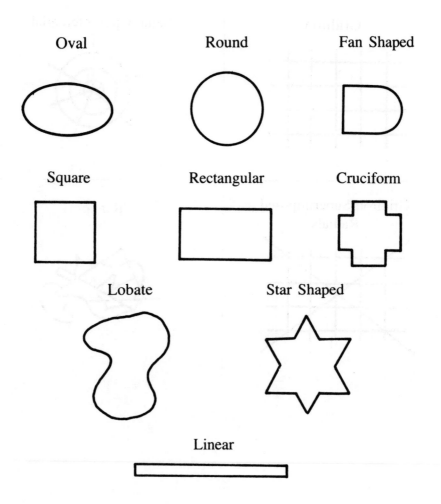

Oval

Round

Fan Shaped

Square

Rectangular

Cruciform

Lobate

Star Shaped

Linear

The diagram above represents possible shape catagories of central cities. Lines of high speed transport have considerable influence on city shape.

METROPOLITAN AREA PATTERN

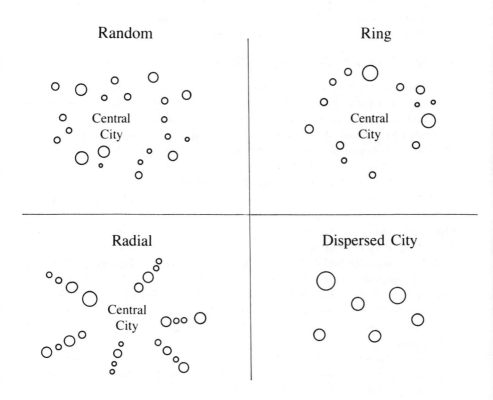

The diagram above represents the possible arrangement of suburbs and sattelite cities around the core of a central city. Random, ring, or radial patterns are obvious, but the "dispersed city" configuration may need a word of explanation. Dispersed cities are a closely spaced group of small cities, of about the same size, that function as a single economic unit. See Hayes, Charles R., *The Dispersed City*, Chicago, The University of Chicago Department of Geography Research Paper No. 173 (1976) for an explanation of this metropolitan configuration.

Figure 11 illustrates possible street patterns and Figure 12 possible central city shapes. The rectangular shapes are usually associated with a gridiron street pattern and the circular shapes with radial or radial-circumferential street patterns. The linear shaped cities often derive shape from a gridiron street pattern along a barrier (i.e. river, ridge, etc.). Combination street patterns may result in some of the other shapes illustrated.

Metropolitan area patterns are strongly influenced by lines of high speed transport whether for public or private vehicles. Figure 13 illustrates possible metropolitan area configuration. It is evident that transport routes have considerable influence on the type of pattern that develops.

Expressways and the Interstate System

The first modern express highways were developed during the 1930s in Germany and Italy. The *autobahen* and *austrada* respectively were originally intended primarily for military movements. The basic design elements were presented to millions of people at the General Motors *Futurama,* a very elaborate series of animated exhibits at the New York World's Fair in 1939-40. At about the same time the first rural express highway in the United States was opened: the original stretch of the Pennsylvania Turnpike, on an expanded right-of-way of an aborted railroad through the Appalachians. But World War II began, and Americans had concerns other than the planning of future highways. However, Congress, fearing that transportation bottlenecks would develop as they did during the earlier World War, commissioned a study for a system of Interstate and Defense Highways. The report, submitted to Congress in 1944, proposed such a system, to connect all regional and almost all metropolitan areas of the nation and drew upon the German and Italian precedents for design criteria. Not entirely coincidentally, the entire network which was proposed very closely resembled that depicted in the General Motors exhibition of a few years earlier.

After the end of the war, automobile ownership and use expanded very rapidly, and the intercity trucking industry, involving common and contract carriers as well as private trucks, diverted a very high proportion of the merchandise and other high-class freight from the railroads while at the same time sharing fully in the overall growth of transportation. The need for more modern highways was clearly evident, and in the summer of 1952 President Eisenhower appealed in a broadcast to the nation to provide a more adequate system of highways; in effect, to activate the program proposed by General Motors in 1939 and by the congressional report of 1944. Shortly thereafter, General Motors announced a nationwide contest for the best essays on the methods of financing and effectuating the Interstate Highway system. Winner of the first prize — not surprisingly — was Robert Moses, who earlier was largely responsible for the system of parkways on Long Island and Westchester County, New York. Moses proposed setting up a trust fund to be devoted exclusively for the purpose, and to tax motor fuel and some other items associated with operation of highway vehicles. The system, as authorized in 1956, was to include 41,500 miles (later increased to about 42,500 miles) of completely grade-separated, limited-access, medially-divided highway, with wide lanes, and gentle horizontal and vertical curves with long sight-distances. The federal government was to provide ninety percent of the cost from the trust fund. The state, county and local governments were to provide the remainder. Originally, no provision was made for federal participation in maintenance costs. The estimated cost in 1956 dollars, was to be about 27 billion, making it the largest single-purpose public works program ever initiated.

With over 95 percent of the system completed by the early 1980s, the cost was over 100 billion dollars, due in part to inflation, in part to addition to the originally proposed system, and in part to increased land and construction costs for the urban portions. Most uncompleted portions of the system are in the more densely developed parts of cities, where costs would be considerably higher, for land acquisition, relocation, clearance and construction, than for the completed portions. In many cities, the originally-planned links have been, in part, "demapped", that is removed from adoption, even though substantial land areas have been purchased and in many instances cleared.

It was originally estimated that the Federal System of Interstate and Defense Highways, constituting about 1.4 percent of the total mileage of the nation's roads and streets, would carry between 20 and 25 percent of the vehicle-miles of traffic. This estimate subsequently proved to essentially correct. The Interstates constitute by far the most important links in the internal circulatory systems of most large and medium sized cities and metropolitan areas in the United States and they have had major effects upon the spatial patterns of land use in nearly all of the urban areas through which they pass, or which they serve.

When the Interstate system was planned little thought was given to prospective impacts upon other transportation systems, especially the railroads. Much high-class freight traffic, especially manufactured goods, moved from the railroads to the highways. Growth of intercity trucks, both in numbers and in size, has been important in increasing the predominance of railroads as primarily bulk haulers of commodities which do not easily, or at all, lend themselves to long-distance highway movement. The inter-city trucking industry grew rapidly, and in an attempt to remain competitive for much of their high-revenue producing traffic, the railroads developed piggybacking, with moderate success.

It was originally believed that the express highways, converging toward cental areas of cities in a radial pattern, would reinforce the dominance of urban cores, many of which were already declining as a result of residential deconcentration, loss of purchasing power in many "inner city" neighborhoods, and the beginnings of the proliferating outlying regional shopping centers, as well as the suburbanization of numerous industrial and office activities. To facilitate access to the "downtowns" circumferential express highways were constructed around the urban cores, complementary to "beltways" or outer circumferentials, which, together with the radials, formed "spiderweb" patterns around many of the larger cities.

Some links in the expressway systems of cities will never be completed. The environmental movement of the late 1960s and early '70s and the mandatory environmental impact studies focused attention on some of the adverse effect on the urban environment of express highways. The fuel crisis of the same period, together with prospects of continued increases in cost, and with possible future decreases in availability of motor fuel resulted in less use of automobiles, and in shrinkage of the size of cars. At the same time, deregulation of the motor trucking industry, in some respects, together with the perceived need for fuel economies, slowed up the rate of growth of truck traffic. The population growth rate, also, has slowed up. The combined effect of these trends has been a decline, throughout the 1970s, of traffic volumes in many urban areas, and, earlier, over-estimation of the need for additonal express highways in some cities. Furthermore, most missing links in the system would be far more expensive than those already built, not only because of escalation of land aquisition and clearance because of relocation of families, businesses and utilities along the rights-of-way, and because of the objections to the disruption of neighborhoods through which the roads would pass. In many instances, rights-of-way were acquired and cleared, leaving vacant swaths for miles. These swaths have contributed to the decline of substantial portions of some cities. There are may instances of aborted construction, and of missing connections resulting in stubs of roads, not connected at their ends. The Embarkadero Freeway on the San Francisco waterfront, and Milwaukee's missing link in the originally proposed downtown loop freeway, as well as a massive bridge across the harbor entrance, unconnected at the south end because the proposed freeway southward is no longer needed, are typical examples.

Many express highways which traverse previously builtup urban areas have disrupted or destroyed otherwise viable neighborhoods. In some instances these areas were inhabited predominantly by minorities, who were forced to relocate, adding additional population pressures and contributing thus to the decline of other portions of the respective cities and metropolitan areas. Small businesses commonly were forced to close as their clientel moved, further contributing to neighborhood decline.

On the other hand, the urban and metropolitan express highway systems reinforced the centrifugal forces leading toward deconcentration. By making more accessible the peripheral areas of cities and the suburban areas beyond, they contributed, and continue to contribute, to the outward movement of population, as well as commercial and industrial establishments. Regional shopping centers, industrial parks, clusters of suburban office buildings, all developed rapidly during and following the period of rapid express highway building. Although it is not possible to isolate the effects of the highways from other factors, there is no doubt that the availability of improved access contributed to the deconcentration of urban activities, by reducing the frictions and costs of overcoming distance, and increasing the accessibility of land on and beyond the urban peripheries.

On the other hand, the increase in employment opportunities in the outer portions of cities and in the suburbs was not generally advantageous to the inner city populations who had depended upon nearby establishments for their employment. Many new foci were, and are, far from the residential areas of unskilled and semi-skilled population, a high proportion of whom cannot afford either automobiles or the expense of using them to commute long distances between home and work. Information as to availability of jobs in peripheral areas is sometimes not readily available to "inner city" residents, and there frequently is an imbalance between the peripheral demand for labor and the location of the available labor force. Many inner city residents, having lost their jobs as a result of the decline of commercial and industrial opportunities through relocation of establishments and differential growth elsewhere, are doubly penalized by their inability to commute or to move to where employment may be greater.

The effects of the expressway systems upon central cities were not fully anticipated when the systems were planned. By stimulating through expressway construction the decentralizating and deconcentration of employment and of residents, cities lost substantial parts of their tax base. Declining property values as population and business moved from the more centrally located areas resulted in lower taxable values, but there were also decreases in sales tax revenues, and, in cities with local wage or income taxes, decreases in those tax revenues also. Because many metropolitan areas have complex spatial patterns of local governments, the economies of scale are often lost through duplication of facilities as population and income decentralize, while leaving behind unused capacity of buildings, utilities, and services. Thus, improved internal transportation may contribute to the fiscal plight of some cities, large and small.

Mass Transit

Mass transit after a long period of decline, is showing signs in the 1970s and early 1980s of a small resurgence in some cities and metropolitan areas. In most places the bus is the only mass transit vehicle, and in nearly every city it is the dominant one. On the other hand, "fixed guideway" modes, after a long period of relative and in most instances absolute decline, are receiving increased attention as the rising cost of automobile transportation continues. The effects upon the spatial patterns of land use are already being felt in some metropolitan areas of the United States and Canada.

During much of the nineteenth century, the horse-drawn omnibus was the principal, and in many cities the only, urban mass transit vehicle. Common carrier service, on fixed routes at regular scheduled intervals, was provided in some cities, but the slowness of internal transportation limited the feasible distance between workplaces and living places, so that cities then were necessarily characterized by high density. A major improvement was the placing of the vehicles on rails, beginning in New York City in 1832. During the 1850s the horse-drawn streetcar spread rapidly, so that by the time of the Civil War it constituted the principal mode of mass transportation in many cities.

The electric street railway first appeared in 1885. By the turn of the century it had generally replaced the horsecar in many urban areas. Streetcar lines were extended beyond the edges of many urbanized areas. The entrepreneurs who developed them hoped to realize substantial profits from the real estate holdings which they acquired where the lines were to provide access. Thus, the street railways were important instruments of urban development and expansion.

In some cities, an interim form of local mass transit was the cable car. Originally developed to overcome the hills in San Francisco, the cable car was present in many cities during the latter third of the nineteenth century, but with the advent of the electric trolley car its era was short-lived. In the United States it survives only in San Francisco where it originated, serving not only as a part of the local transit system, but also as a world-famous tourist attraction.

Electric street railways, for many years, were typically owned and operated by private interests having frandises to use the city streets, in return for which the operators agreed to maintain the street pavement between the rails in good condition. In many instances parallel streetcar lines competed with each other, but in time mergers of the companies achieved a certain amount of unification of the local transit systems, which, with some exceptions, continued largely under private ownership.

The streetcars generally operated on the major arterial streets, in radial and grid patterns. At major intersections — the "transfer corners" — outlying business clusters developed growing outward along the radiating streets, and typically forming cross-shaped outlines, the arms characterized by lower densities with distance from the respective intersections.

Since the street cars could stop frequently, the street frontages along their routes were also expected to develop with commercial retail and service establishments, in the form of more-or-less continuous ribbons. In many instances such patterns did, in effect, emerge, but in other instances they did not. In such places, the land fronting on the arterial streets having transit lines was not needed for commercial use. Residential development tended not to take place, because of higher land costs attributed to the often misleading expectations of commercial use, while at the same time the frequent passing of the streetcars close to the properties made then less desirable for residence, even though residential development was stimulated by them a block or two away from their routes. Zoning, which was adopted by many cities in the 1920s and subsequently, exacerbated the problem of frontage along the arterials having street cars, by providing for strip or ribbon zoning of far greater areas than the nearby residential neighborhoods could justify. The later general use of automobiles spelled the demise of many such commercial ribbons, because parking was inadequate at curbside, and because it was not long before the modern planned shopping nucleations became common. Nevertheless, hundreds of miles of such ribbons remain, in many cities, and still form conspicuous elements of the urban land use pattern. Typically, they embrace extensive areas of vacant land which either was never used, or which suffered from declining use, high vacancy rates in the buildings along the streets, and eventual demolition. As the higher and middle income households developed on and beyond the urban peripheries, the declining purchasing power adjacent to many older commercial ribbons brought about decline, deterioration and, in some instances, abandonment.

The heyday of the street railway was in the early years of the twentieth century. Except in a very few cities with rapid transit elevated and subway lines, the streetcar was the sole means of mass transportation other than commuter services on some of the intercity railroads. In 1912, for example, the street railways of the United States carried over eleven *billion* passenger rides or about 93 percent of all transit passengers in the nation. By 1920 rides reached 13.7 billion, but because of the opening of additional rapid transit lines in a few of the largest cities, the nationwide total of streetcar rides declined to 88 percent of all mass transit rides. Subsequently, patronage of the street railways never again reached the earlier peaks of the period of World War I and the early 1920s. The bus soon replaced the streetcar as the major mass transit vehicle, and more significantly, the automobile replaced both streetcar and bus mass transit in most cities as the dominant mode of internal transportation. Nevertheless, the streetcar left its heritage in the form of major elements of the land use pattern in the areas of cities which had significant growth and change, both centrally located and on the then peripheries.

A variant of the streetcar for about fifty years was the interurban electric railway. These railways operated, as did the streetcars, with electric power. Most had overhead transmission wires, although some used third rails for power distribution. The rolling stock was usually heavier than the typical streetcars, although toward the end of the interurban era, in attempts to reduce costs and achieve somewhat higher speeds, some electric interurban railways operated in the streets of the built-up areas of cities, in some instances sharing tracks with the local street railways. In suburban and rural areas they commonly operated on their own rights-of-way, much as the steam railroads did, although with few exceptions the interurban routes were of lighter construction.

Following the first interurban electric railway in the United States, seven miles of which opened in 1889, they proliferated and expanded rapidly, with more than a thousand miles constructed in each year between 1901 and 1908, except for 1905 when 696 miles were built. There was little further construction after World War I, and in 1927 the last 34 miles were opened. The peak year of the electric interurban, route mileage was 1916, when over 15 thousand miles of routes were in operation. By that time, competition, not only from the steam railroads, but also from automobiles, and shortly thereafter from buses, was increasing. Abandonments of the interurban electric railways rapidly accelerated. Over a thousand miles were discontinued in each year during the depression of the early 1930s. In 1963 the last interurban electric railway gave up; the few remaining lines had been essentially converted to conventional railroads, depending upon freight for their principal revenues.

In some metropolitan areas the interurbans left distinctive imprints upon the spatial patterns of land use. Whereas the conventional railroads with commuter service had stimulated a pattern of radial tentacles of urbanization, with nucleii — the commercial and higher-density residential cores of suburban communities — spaced at intervals along their routes, where train stops were located — the interurbans tended to produce more continuous radial axes of suburban development along their lines. The reason was that the interurban cars — on some lines operated as multiple-unit trains — could stop more frequently without significantly reducing overall transit time, because of more rapid acceleration and deceleration than possible with conventional locomotive-hauled trains. Thus there were, in many instances, a filling in between the older suburban nucleii, where the electric interurbans paralleled the commuter services of conventional railroads. But the interurbans could not compete with improved highways and they fell victims to the changing technology and the ubiquity of the private vehicle.

The earliest steam railroads in the United States carried people between their residences in the countryside and nearby towns to their places of work in the cores of the cities. In order to assure adequate traffic on intercity trains, fares for short-distance travelers who rode regularly were "commuted": offered at lower price than the fares paid by less frequent travelers. The first trains specifically operated and scheduled for commuters were on the New York and Harlem Railroad in 1832, and the idea spread to many cities in the northeast as they gained rail service. In Chicago, commuter trains operated to the north, west, and south in the 1850s.

Because the trains operated at much higher speeds than could the local transit services within the cities, the distance that city workers could live from their places of work — which had been very close to the urban centers — increased dramatically. Of course, only the relatively affluent originally could afford to commute by railroad. The result was that the suburban residential developments were inhabited mainly by the more well-to-do. Around the stations along the radiating railroads which provided commuter service, there tended to develop clusters of local business, as well as residential areas, the latter within walking distance, or easy carriage distance, of the outlying railroad stations. The latter formed chains, like beads on a string, along the radiating railroad routes.

The advent of electric power resulted in some suburban commuter services shifting to either locomotive-hauled electric trains, or to multiple-unit trains, in which motors on each car or alternate cars were controlled by an operator at the head-end of the train. The same multiple-unit principle was adopted by some electric interurban railways at about the same time. The new elevated and subway rapid transit lines in several eastern cities and in Chicago either were constructed for multiple-unit train operation or were converted from steam. Multiple-unit electric trains made possible not only subways, but also the air-rights developments over terminals, as in mid-Manhattan.

The term "rapid transit" refers to passenger services operated on rights-of-way separated from other traffic, as distinguished from street operation on the one hand, and suburban commuter trains on the other. Within cities, separation involves either elevation above the level of the streets, or depression in open cuts or in subways. The first elevated rapid transit lines were opened in New York City in the 1870s. Chicago's first elevated transit lines were operated by steam following their opening in 1893, but they, and others soon to follow, were provided with electric power shortly thereafter, and the "Loop", after which Chicago's downtown was named, connected the radiating elevated lines in 1897. In addition to New York and Chicago, several other American cities were provided with elevated rapid transit lines during the 1890s and the first two decades of the twentieth century.

These lines were generally laid on steel trestles, either above the streets or, as in the case of Chicago's South Side line, in the alleys. In either case, the structures were unsightly, they deprived ground areas and nearby structures of light, and the trains were generally noisy. Before electrification, the steam trains caused air pollution from the particulate matter emitted by the coal-fired locomotives, and sparks sometimes caused fires. Land values along the streets traversed by the elevated railroads were depressed although in the vicinities of the stations, and at distances more than a few hundred yards from the lines the access provided by the "L"'s stimulated both commercial and apartment residential developments, with consequent substantial increases in land values.

In spite of the access which they provided, the rapid transit elevated railroads did not solve the problems of internal movement within the cities that had them. They could only serve portions of such cities, and, furthermore, their detrimental aspects made them unpopular. It was clear that another form of intra-city rapid transit was needed in the larger urban areas. Fortunately, a technical solution was available, in the form of multiple-unit train operation, which was already being applied to the elevated lines. In spite of high construction costs and disruption to the city's activities when "cut and cover" construction was used, subways were built in Boston, New York, and Philadelphia around the turn of the century. The first was in Boston, where trolley cars were operated underground through the center of the city as early as 1897. New York's first subway, with four parallel tracks, opened in 1904. Chicago did not begin operation of its first underground portion of the rapid transit system until 1943. Following completion of additional lines in New York in 1932, there was a hiatus in subway construction until the late 1950s; subsequently subway lines were placed under construction in the metropolitan areas of San Francisco-Oakland, Washington, Atlanta, Baltimore, and Buffalo, among other cities.

Subway lines, like elevated rapid transit lines, transfer land values to the vicinities of the stations, but, unlike the elevated lines, do not have adverse effects which are reflected in lower land values in their immediate vicinities once construction is completed. Although it is sometimes difficult to determine whether the rapid rise in land values, and the developments which accompany or follow them, would occur in a different and perhaps less concentrated pattern were the transit lines not to be built, transit has always been used, among other purposes, as a stimulant to development along their routes.

The motor bus, by far the predominant mode of intra-city mass transit, became fairly common during the 1920s, and proliferated after World War II. Originally regarded as most useful in extending the transit services beyond the ends of the trolley and rapid transit lines where low densities made rail service impracticable, the bus soon was regarded as a more desirable substitute for the street railways. It has many advantages; among them are freedom from routes fixed by rails and electric transmission lines and consequently the ability to detour around obstacles and obstructions, loading and discharging passengers at curbside instead of the middle of the street, elimination of need to maintain rails, power lines, transformer substations, and pavement between the rails, and the ability to service lines with light traffic density where the costs of building and maintaining rails and transmission lines are not justified. On the other hand, buses, burning petroleum fuel, create air pollution, and their weaving through traffic may cause delays to automobiles, trucks and other vehicles in the traffic stream. A counterbalancing advantage is that, lacking substantial investment in fixed routes, the vehicles can be shifted about as the activity patterns of land uses of the city change.

The rise of the motor bus as the principal form of intra-city mass transit was very rapid after World War II. In 1940, when street cars were still in operation in many cities, buses carried 32.36 percent of all local transit passengers. By 1945 this had increased to 42.51 percent and a decade later to 54.62 percent. By 1975 the proportion of all city transit passengers moved by bus was 72.92. All of these percentages would be substantially higher if the very largest cities — especially New York — which have elevated and subway rapid transit lines, were excluded.

On the other hand, mass transit in general has greatly decreased in importance as a mover of people within cities and metropolitan areas, both relatively and absolutely. In 1940 all forms of mass transit — rail, trolley coach, and bus — together carried 13.1 billion passengers, and in 1945, when automobile transportation was restricted by wartime and immediate postwar conditions, transit riding peaked at 23.3 billion passengers. Since then, use of mass transit declined steadily until 1972, when only 6.6 billion passengers were carried. The increased price and uncertain availability of motor fuel, and the escalating cost of automobiles during the 1970s was reflected in a "bottoming out" of the decline in mass transit use. In the late 1970s there was a slight increase in number of transit passengers annually. During 1980 and 1981, however, the increase slowed up, due in part to the business recession and in part to the rising costs of mass transit, brought about both in cost of fuel and other supplies as well as the rapidly rising labor costs. Bus operation is labor-intensive.

A relatively unimportant mode of mass transit is the trolley coach, or "trackless trolley". This mode, introduced in the 1920s, never achieved wide-spread popularity, but is witnessing a small revival in the early 1980s. Its peak was about 1950 when, in many cities, it had replaced some of the electric street railway lines, and in some instances was extended beyond the ends of rapid transit routes. The trolley coach combines some of the advantages of the electric streetcar, and some of the flexibility of the bus but without the disad-vantage of rail operation, but nevertheless with fixed routes because of the transmission lines. From 1950, when the trackless trolley moved 1.3 billion passengers, it declined steadily to 55.8 million passengers in 1975. In a few cities, such as Seattle, the increased price of motor fuel is largely responsible for restoration of trolley coaches on some routes where they had previously been replaced by motor buses.

Much more important is the resurgence of rail rapid transit in a number of metropolitan areas of the United States and Canada during the 1960s and subse-quently. During the seventies the rapidly rising costs of automobile operation added incentive to plans for rapid transit systems, not only as extensions and additional lines in cities which already had rapid transit, but also as major local transportation facilities in cities and metropolitan areas which previously depended entirely upon streetcar, and, later, bus, operation for their local mass transit.

Since World War II rail rapid transit had lost much of its former impor-tance, even in the few cities and metropolitan areas which had it. In 1945 rail transit lines carried 9.6 billion passengers, or just over half of all local transit passengers in the nation. By 1975 rail transit's share of the national transit passenger movement was only 24 percent, nearly all of which was on elevated and subway line. The trolley car was almost extinct, carrying only about 1.7 percent of all transit passengers. Only a handful of cities had street railway lines remaining.

With increasing costs and the inexorable advance of automobile transpor-tation, transit operators found it increasingly difficult to meet their costs, not to mention profit. In city after city, the transit companies folded, or were taken over and supplanted by public agencies. In some cities, such as Chicago, bank-rupt streetcar, bus and rapid transit companies were merged into a public authority. In New York City the rapid transit and many bus routes were taken over by a municipal authority and subsequently by a state agency, the Metropolitan Transit Authority, which also owns and operates the Long Island

Railroad, the nation's largest carrier of suburban commuters.

It became clear that transit operation was — and is — in the public interest. Automobiles are inefficient, not only in their use of energy, but also in the amount of land used to accommodate them, both in motion and at rest. Cities could not afford the costs of the automobile in terms of congestion, absorption of land both in streets and offstreets, in emission-caused air pollution, and in the lower densities of fringe development both necessitated by and encouraging the use of the automobile. The interest in mass transit was greatly reinforced by the fuel crisis in 1967 and again in the 1970s. Although fuel-efficient automobiles are increasingly coming into use, with prospects for further fuel economies in the future as a result of improved engines and smaller cars, and although automobile usage has somewhat declined because of increasing costs, the automobile will remain the dominant mode of urban and suburban passenger transportation in the foreseeable future. The dominance of the automobile relative to mass transit is demonstrated by Table 2.

TABLE 4

MEANS OF TRANSPORTATION TO WORK, BY RESIDENCE, 1975 (Percent)

Means of Transportation	Inside SMSAs — Inside Central cities	Inside SMSAs — Outside central cities	Outside SMSAs
Automobile and truck	77.14	88.62	87.53
Drive alone	59.85	69.68	67.28
Carpool	17.29	13.94	22.08
Public transportation	14.01	4.40	0.81
Bus or streetcar	8.91	2.83	0.88
Subway or elevated train	4.56	0.43	-
Railroad	0.23	1.05	0.04
Taxicab	0.32	0.12	0.35
Other means	1.27	1.37	1.34
Walked only	5.96	3.44	5.25
Worked at home	1.62	2.17	6.10

SOURCE: Compled from: U.S. Bureau of the Census, *Current Population Reports, series P-23, No. 99* and unpublished data, as reported in: U.S. Bureau of the Census, *Statistical Abstract of the United States 1980,* table 113, p. 657.

TRANSPORTATION EXPENDITURE

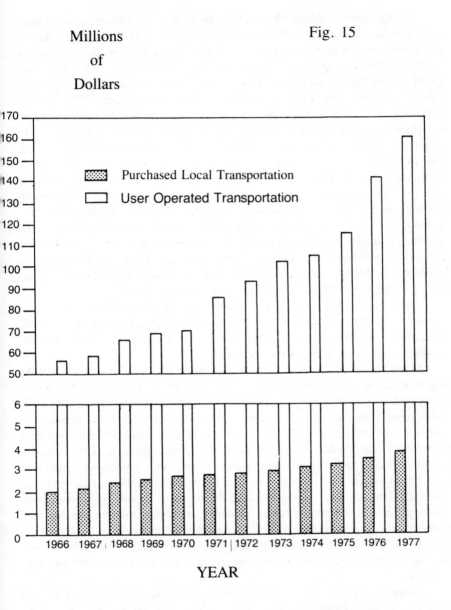

Millions
of
Dollars

Fig. 15

The graph above shows the ever widening gap between user operated transportation and purchased transportation. Although the truck made industrial counter-urbanization feasible, the private auto permits human counter-urbanization.

The first new rapid transit system to be built in the United States in sixty years was the San Francisco Bay Area Rapid Transit (BART). In 1962 voters in San Francisco and in Alameda and Contra Costa counties on the east side of San Francisco Bay approved a bond issue of $792 million, by the Bay Area Rapid Transit District, with additional revenues to come from Bay Bridge tolls, federal agencies, the State legislature and passenger fares. The system, consisting of 75 miles of double track, including a four-mile transbay tunnel and three branches in the East Bay, was designed to take advantage of the advances in the ''state of the art'' since the last previously built transit system was designed, more than six decades earlier. Although there were some technological difficulties soon after BART's initial portions were placed in operation, the system has been successful in competing with highway transportation in those portions of the metropolitan area which it serves. However, only between three and four percent of the daily trips are handled by BART, and automobile traffic has not noticeably been reduced since the system became available. Subsequently, extensive rapid transit lines were opened in Washington (Metro) and Atlanta metropolitan areas (MARTA), and others placed under construction in Baltimore, Buffalo, and Miami.

The earlier rapid transit lines, and most of those mentioned above, are ''heavy rail'' systems, characterized by complete separation from street traffic by multiple-unit trains, and control of the train intervals by signal devices, although automation is extensively utilized.

Many more cities are interested in providing a form of rail transit, but the potential traffic, or the financial resources, or both, are not sufficient to justify heavy rail. In such instances, ''light rail'' is regarded as a partial answer. Light rail is, essentially, an advanced version of the old-fashioned street railway, but with some of the characteristics of heavy rail. These include multiple-unit train operation — at least during peak periods —, signalling, in some instances regular stations rather than street-corner stops, and, commonly, extensive stretches of private right-of-way with trackage resembling those of conventional railroads. Portions may be on elevated structures or in subway. Street grade crossings, however, may occur in places. Cars are of modern design, with many features that were absent on the earlier street railway cars. In some cities, such as Edmonton, Alberta, and Buffalo, New York, the light rail lines are in subway in the more densely built-up areas including the central business districts.

Integration of the rail transit lines with other modes is essential if the rail lines are to serve extensive areas of the cities. Such integration, physically, consists of ''park and ride'' areas, where the automobile can remain while the commuter proceeds to and from work — or other destinations — by rail, and ''kiss and ride'' areas where an automobile driver can discharge and pick up passengers before and after the transit ride without parking. Commonly, the transit stations have provision for interchange of riders with bus lines, thereby greatly extending the service areas of the rail facilities. In many instances, these parking and station areas occupy the equivalent of several city blocks, and the pedestrian passenger may be required to walk a considerable distance before and after the train ride, across the terminal areas. One solution, which has been adopted in some instances, is non-transportational structures over the rail stations; these may be office buildings, high-rise apartment, retail stores or theatres, in addition to parking garages. These high-density developments may further stimulate others thereby creating substantial outlying — or central — nucleii associated with the high-density transportation facilities.

Much of the stimulus for the resurgence of rapid transit and light rail in American cities has been the federal government, which provided up to eighty percent of the cost of such systems or of extensions and improvement to earlier systems. While federal aid was by no means confined to rail systems (but purchases and operation also received federal subsidies) the extremely costly modes could generally not have been built without federal financial participation. The "new federalism" initiated in 1981 raises the possibility that fewer, if any, rail transit system other than those already committed will subsequently be initiated in the cities and metropolitan areas of the United States. In any event, the funds contributed by the federal government has been small relative to the vast amounts devoted to the federal highway programs.

Urban and metropolitan mass transit, including both bus and rail, rarely, if ever, can be self-supporting from user fares. In a sense, transit represents an addition to street capacity. It has the additional advantage of reducing the need for land devoted to extensive parking areas, especially in high-density destination areas, such as central business districts and other major foci, where land costs are very high. In such areas a much greater economic return can be realized from non-transportational uses which depend upon the access provided by all modes, but particularly, public transit.

With the virtual impossibility of meeting costs from revenues, transit cannot attract private venture capital. More and more transit companies either went bankrupt and discontinued operations, or were taken over and supplanted by public agencies. An additional incentive for public ownership and/or operation or urban and metropolitan transit systems was the availability of federal and state funding for construction. Urban transit systems are public systems. In some instances, the transit agency is a municipality or a county, in others a state agency, and in a few metropolitan areas an interstate agency, either a specialized transit agency or a general authority such as a port district, may have the responsibility for the transit system.

The Automobile

The almost ubiquitous automobile was largely responsible for the decline of transit systems. Not only is automobile ownership almost a necessity in most metropolitan areas and cities, but it is a major constituent of most peoples' life style. During most of the twentieth century it has been a principal force in shaping the spatial pattern of land uses in virtually every city. In spite of escalating costs of purchasing, maintaining and operating private cars, and in spite of the long-range pessimistic outlook for continued availability and high cost of motor fuel, there is little doubt that the private automobile, in one form or another, will continue its dominant role, since it provides door-to-door service, and is unmatched in convenience by any other mode of transportation. Of the more than 150 million motor vehicles registered in the United States in 1980, over 120 million were passenger cars. The number doubled in the two decades between 1960 and 1980 and has tripled since 1950. The number and extent of use of automobiles have far outpaced the provision for them, in spite of highway construction and the many parking facilities provided in the more congested areas of cities.

Critics of the automobile point out that it is a very inefficient user of space, of energy, and of income. They assert that mass transit could and should be developed to a greater extent than at present, in order to relieve pressures on the land in congested areas, as well as to reduce other adverse effects of motor vehicles such as air pollution.

The importance of the automobile in American cities is witnessed by the fact that there are fifty percent more automobiles than households in the nation. The significance of suburbanization in automobile ownership is shown by the greater preponderance of cars in the metropolitan suburbs than in the central cities: in suburbs in 1977 90.9 percent of households had one or more cars, as compared with 72 percent in the central cities. Multiple-car households constitute 44.6 percent of all suburban households, while in the central cities only 26.2 percent of households had two or more cars. With increases in households, with two or more income earners especially in the central cities, the role of mass transit in taking up the slack should increase. There is a high correlation between income and multiple-car ownership; a higher proportion of central city as compared with suburban residents cannot afford to own more than one car, if that.

The automobile is equally used for commuting and work-related trips on one hand, and family and personal business trips, other than for civic, educational, religious, social and recreational on the other hand. About one-third of the total car use is for each of these three purposes. The average distance of a commuting trip is about 9.2 miles; less in metropolitan areas than in rural areas.

Metropolitan Transportation Land Use Studies

The close reciprocal relationship between transportation on the one hand and land use on the other was not fully realized until relatively recently. Of course, access was, and always will be, an indispensable prerequisite to land development and use, but planners generally until the 1950s, tended to conduct transportation research separate from research on land use. Now, the investigations of the reciprocal roles constitutes a vital part of the planning process.

During the early decades of the twentieth century, the need for improved roads was so obvious that the supply could scarcely keep up with the demand. Virtually every road improvement was useful so detailed studies of demand were not vital. On the other hand, traffic counts were frequently conducted, often by sampling, and the results were commonly in the form of flow maps. Each route segment was represented as a band, the width of which was proportional to the traffic passing over a segment, or counted at a point, within a given period of time: a year, a day, or a peak hour. The flows were then compared with theoretical formulae indicating the capacities of streets and roads with various lanes, lane widths, intersections etc., and with observations of bottlenecks where the actual traffic, especially during peak times, exceeded the actual or theoretical capacity. Improvements were then planned to relieve the bottlenecks, insofar as financial and physical conditions permitted. These improvements included widenings, provision of additional lanes, one-way traffic, turning lanes and, in some instances, grade separation at major intersections. Less radical and costly improvements frequently resolved some of the capacity problems. These included changes in the signal intervals, better channelization, restrictions of on-street parking, and other changes involving minimum capital expenditures.

The traffic flow studies, however, showed only the contemporary movement patterns; they did not furnish any indications of where the movements between origins and destinations would take place if more adequate and more direct routes were available.

During the 1940s and 1950s, the Bureau of Public Roads (now the Federal Highway Administration in the U.S. Department of Transportation) developed a technique, which was generally used in studies of many metropolitan areas, for conducting origin-destination (O-D) traffic studies. These studies divided an areas into zones and subzones of several degrees of magnitude within a so-called cordon; a line surrounding the study area, which generally was a major part of a metroplitan complex, in which all trips made by household members on the previous day — usually a typical weekday, with no unusual local events or weather conditions, — were tabulated by zones of origin and zones of destination. Traffic crossing the cordon was subjected to an "external" survey, in which a sample of the travelers was asked for information similar to that supplied by the internal home interview sample. Transit operators, taxicabs, and truck operators were surveyed also. Information was gathered on the age, sex, occupation, and other attributes of each of the persons making a trip, and on the time of the day, vehicular mode, transfers if any, and purpose of each trip. Cross-tabulations of any of these variables were then possible. Fortunately, these surveys were conducted initially at the time when electronic data processing was first becoming available, and major O-D traffic studies in the mid 1950s in Detroit, Chicago, Pittsburgh, and Philadelphia, among other areas, were the first large planning programs to make use of the newer information-handling technologies.

The reports of these O-D surveys include maps of "desire lines" which are straight lines between zones of origin and zones of destination, regardless of the routes actually taken. These desire line maps indicated not only total trips — based upon expansion of the selected samples — but also trips made at various periods of time, for various purposes, by different modes, and by individuals catagorized by their age, sex, occupation and other characteristics. The resultant desire lines were then compared with the actual routes and where they did not coincide, there were indications of the potential traffic on new routes that could be built and developed. The "boom" in highway construction at that time, soon to be reinforced by the development of the Federal System of Interstate and Defense Highways authorized by the Highway Act of 1956, made the O-D surveys very useful in planning the locations and alignments of the many urban and metropolitan portions of the new roads, and, later, of transit routes as well.

A major publication in 1954 *(Urban Traffic: A Function of Land Use*, by Robert B. Mitchell and Chester A. Rapkin, Columbia University Press) pointed out that planning of local transportation systems previously had been seriously deficient in not adequately relating traffic to the spatial patterns of land use, which, after all, are responsible for the generation of the traffic. It became clearly evident that projection of increases in traffic with increasing population and activity were inadequate bases for provision of additional facilities; that the locations, densities, and spatial patterns of land uses were very important, and that one could not assume growth of traffic demand without considering the prospective changes in the patterns of land use which would inevitably produce changes in the spatial patterns of traffic. The authors emphasized the necessity of relating land use and traffic patterns to each other, and to plan comprehensively with due regard to their mutual impacts.

The Highway Act of 1956, authorizing the Interstate system, was implemented by construction of thousands of miles of express highways through metropolitan areas. They involved, in some instances, expenditures of hundreds of millions of dollars per mile, including land acquisition, relocations of residents and business establishments, demolition, replacement of utilities along the routes, and commonly, expensive and protracted litigation before the land acquisition could begin. In this process, the O-D surveys were very useful in establishing the supposed need for the route segments.

At the same time, procedures were devised and initiated for expansion of the O-D survey concepts to include projections of land-use patterns, and hence refining of the surveys to include alternative patterns ("scenarios") of locations of the "traffic generators" or clusters of land uses by O-D zones. In other words, the O-D traffic surveys evolved into comprehensive transportation-land use surveys, which became integral parts of the process of preparing and revising of comprehensive city and metropolitan plans. By use of the surveys, it was possible, within broad limits, to anticipate the spatial interactions among various land uses, at various distances apart, and with various characteristics, based upon the survey data projected into the future involving consideration of alternative spatial patterns, from which it could be determined which among the alternatives would be most efficient from the viewpoint of minimizing future investment in the handling of movements generated by the alternative spatial land use patterns.

As discussed elsewhere, the Demonstration Cities and Metropolitan Development Act of 1966 required that, as prerequisite for transfer funds from the federal government to the various states, and through the states to local governments, comprehensive planning was to be carried on by regional planning agencies in the metropolitan areas, each such agency to be designated by the State. The general scope and content of such planning was to be determined by the appropriate federal agencies — mostly the Department of Housing and Urban Development and the Department of Transportation. This was implemented by HUD Directive A - 95 which described in general the items to be included, and the general procedures to be followed. The land use and transportation aspects were — and are — regarded as integral parts of the comprehensive plans and any major projects or programs were required to be referred to the metropolitan planning agencies for conformance to the comprehensive plan. Any applications for federal funding were regarded unfavorably unless this conformance was assured.

Partly as a result of these official procedures, a general uniformity and comparability of land use and transportation data among the various metropolitan areas came about, and comparative studies nation-wide became a possibility. The mandate, along with federal participation in the funding of the comprehensive planning process in accordance with Section 701 of the Housing Act of 1954, combined to greatly stimulate metropolitan planning. The implementation of comprehensive planning, as distinguished from the adoption of specific programs and projects, however, was greatly inhibited in most areas because of the absence of metropolitan governments capable of carrying out major elements of the comprehensive plans.

Before any major transportation program or project — or, for that matter, any major program or project — could be carried out, it is required to be preceeded by a detailed environmental impact study, under the provisions of the EPA Act of 1969. Such impact statements are mandated to include alternative solutions to the problems including, in most instances, the alternative of doing nothing. In the development of such impact studies, much useful research has been conducted and, in general, the relations between transportation on the one hand and land use on the other are more clearly understood than was formerly the case.

How the "new federalism" of the administration which took office in

METROPOLITAN AREA
GROWTH PATTERNS

Fig. 16

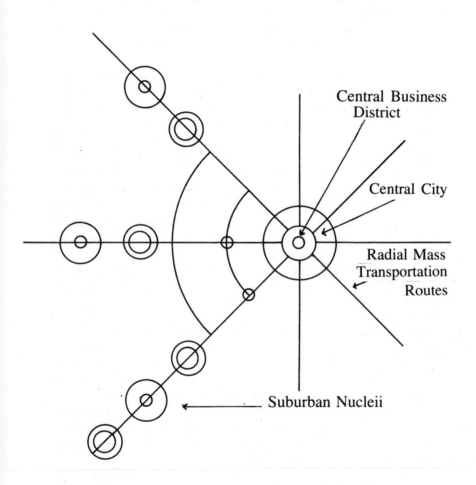

The diagram above is a generalization of the typical growth pattern of a metropolitan area. It also suggests one possible configuration of the relative locations of central city, suburbs, and sattelites. Compare this diagram with Fig. 2 (Urban Growth Models) and Fig. 14 Metropolitan Area Patterns). The diagram is modified from Mayer, Harold M, *The Spatial Expression of Urban Growth*, Resource Paper No. 7, Washington, D.C., Association of American Geographers (1969) p. 40.

1981 will affect these programs of research and planning was not completely resolved by 1982. However, the transportation-land use relationships will undoubtedly, whatever bureaucratic forms the planning process may or may not include, be much more studied and considered than they were in earlier decades.

SELECTED READINGS

A. EXTERNAL TRANSPORTATION AND TERMINALS

Chinitz, Benjamin. *Freight and the Metropolis.* Cambridge, Mass.: Harvard University Press, (1960), pp. 211

Condit, Carl W., *The Port of New York: A History of the Rail and Terminal System.* Chicago: The University of Chicago Press, 2 vols., (1980 and 1981).

Condit, Carl W., *The Railroad and the City, A Technological and Urbanistic History of Cincinnati.* Columbus: Ohio State University Press, (1977).

de Neufville, Richard, *Airport Systems Planning.* Cambridge, Mass.: The M.I.T. Press, (1976).

Hurst, Michael E. Eliot, *Transportation Geography: Comments and Readings.* New York: McGraw-Hill Book Co., (1974).

Mayer, Harold M., "Changing Railroad Patterns in Major Gateway Cities", in: John W. Frazier and Bart J. Epstein (editors), *Applied Geography Conferences,* Vol. 2 (1979), Binghamton, N.Y.: Dept. of Geography, State Univ. of N.Y. at Binghamton, p. 106-122.

Mayer, Harold M., "Transportation Facilities Planning: External", in: Wm. H. Claire (editor), *Handbook on Urban Planning.* New York: Van Nostrand Reinhold Company, (1973), pp. 195-257.

National Transportation Policy Study Commission, *National Transportation Policies Through the Year 2000, Final Report.* Washington: U.S. Government Printing Office, (June 1979), (especially pp. 69-170 and 237-268).

Schenker, Eric and Harry C. Brockel (editors), *Port Planning and Development as Related to Problems of U.S. Ports and the U.S. Coastal Environment.* Cambridge, Maryland: Cornell Maritime Press, (1974).

Smith, Wilbur and Associates, *Motor Trucks in the Metropolis.* Detroit: Automobile Manufacturers Association, (1969).

B. Internal Circulation and Urban Transportation Systems

Altshuler, Alan with James P. Womack and John R. Pucher, *the Urban Transportation System, Politics and Policy Innovation.* Cambridge, Mass.: The M.I.T. Press, (1979), pp. 1084 and 374-471.

Betz, Matthew J., "Land-Use Density, Pattern, and Scale as Factors in Urban Transportation," *Traffic Quarterly*, Vol. 32, No. 2 (April 1978), pp. 263-272.

Boyce, David E. *et. al.*, *Metropolitan Plan Making*, Philadelphia: Regional Science Research Institute, (1970), (especially Chapt. 3) "Review of Land Use and Transportation Programs," pp. 29-81.

Dickey, John W. *et. al.*, *Metropolitan Transportation Planning*, Washington: Scripa Book Co. (McGraw-Hill) (1975), 562 pp., (especially pp. 1-108).

Goetsch, Herbert A., "Transportation Facilities Planning: Internal," Chap. 8 of: Wm. H. Claire (editor), *Handbook on Urban Planning*, New York: Van Nostrand Reinhold Co., (1973), pp. 258-270.

Grant, Albert A., "Use of Origin-Destination Data in Determining Urban Needs," *Traffic Quarterly*, Vol. 24, No. 2 (April 1970) pp. 219-230.

Gray, George E. and Lester A. Hoel (editors), *Public Transportation; Planning, Operations and Management*. Englewood Cliffs, N.J.: Prentice-Hall, Inc., (1979), pp. 4-323 and 662-716.

Krueckeberg, Donald A. and Arthur L. Silvers, *Urban Planning Analysis: Methods and Models*, New York: John Wiley & Sons, Inc., (1974), (Chap. 10), Land Use and Transportation Models," pp. 318-361.

Mayer, Harold M., "Urban Geography and Urban Transportation Planning," *Traffic Quarterly*, Vol. 17, No. 4 (October 1963), pp. 610-631.

Mazey, Mary Ellen, "Extermination of the Distance Component of Urban Activity Space," *Geographical Survey*, Bal State University, Vol. 9, No. 4 (October, 1980), pp. 20-29.

Meyer, J.R., J.F. Kain, and M. Wohl, *The Urban Transportation Problem*, Harvard University Press, (1965).

Mitchell, Robert B. and Chester Rapkin, *Urban Traffic, A Function of Land Use*, New York: Columbia University Press, (1954), 226 pp.

Pushkarev, Boris S. and Jeffrey M. Zupan, *Public Transportation and Land Use Policy*, Bloomington, Ind.: Indiana University Press, (1977), 242 pp. (especially pp. 112 and 172-199).

So, Frank *et. al.* (editors). *The Practice of Local Government Planning.* Washington: International City Management Association, (1979), (Chap. 8: "Urban Transportation." by Alan M. Voohees, Walter G. Hansen and A. Keith Gilbert), pp. 214-245.

Taaffe, Edward J., Howard L. Gauthier, and Thomas A. Maraffa, "Extended Commuting and the Intermetropolitan Periphery," *Annals of the Association of American Geographers,* Vol. 70, No. 3 (September, 1980), pp. 313-329.

Wheeler, James O., *The Urban Circulation Noose,* North Scituate, Mass.: Duxbury Press, (1974), 137 pp.

Index